Teachings of An Outlaw Witch: A Primer for the Curious

Lady Kali Tara

DEDICATION

This work is dedicated to the ancients, our ancestors, teachers, shamans, wise women and medicine men, my daughter, Krista, and my husband, Marcus, who walks the path with me.

.

CONTENTS

ACKNOWLEDGMENTS

Many thanks to my family, teachers, friends, and covens for your support and encouragement.

Beneath the Blessing Moon a promise was made and kept by one who walked a path well worn. Her footsteps soft on the field grass, she stood at the trail's end, basking in the silver rays of The Lady's smile. Chalice in hand, the priestess sipped of the cup, then spilled wine upon the land. Dropping to one knee, she gave thanks to The Lady, The Lord, and all the good elements and elementals of the universe. She placed bread upon the land. Pines whispered approval, while strong oaks stood witness. Fireflies and fairy lights danced upon the breeze. She drew breath and tasted the sweetness of the night. And though she stood at the trail's end, she smiled knowing her walk, her path, had just begun.

Notes of a priestess

Preface

Welcome and What to Expect

So, what is a Haitian/Black/Native-American woman doing writing a book on Wicca? Loving it! Wicca is truly a religion that embraces my eclectic heritage and its diverse beliefs. My path to *The Path* was more direct than you might think. I come from a family with roots in Vodou and witchcraft, as well as more "traditional" religious practices. Most importantly, it is a family that supports the need for each individual to find her way and define her spiritual path. Why write *Teachings of an*

Outlaw Witch? Well, let's just say, although my family proved very accepting, not all whom I encountered were sure that some of the more powerful aspects of my heritage were suited to The Craft. I had wonderful teachers and a dedicated High Priestess, but in the end we didn't agree on all aspects of diversity. We parted; each prepared to follow our paths toward and for the greatest good. My path became the apparently "outlaw" path of an integration of Vodou and the name of Kali, an oft misunderstood Hindu goddess. This book is my choice to teach about a sense of self-empowerment and acceptance that allows you to discover your true nature, the light and shadow aspects of self, and revel in the wholeness of you!

Wicca embraces religious diversity in the sense that it allows for the integration of different cultural beliefs. Let's always keep in mind that with those different cultural beliefs come people of different cultures. We don't necessarily see the same face of diversity in the practice, and I think it's important to know that Wicca is open to people of all colors and cultures, and of equal importance, people of all colors and cultures are practicing Wicca. Whether you are beginning your own quest or simply curious, an understanding of the magick that is Wicca is invaluable. You will learn about the religion, but you'll also learn the strength behind the religion, a strength founded upon acceptance, connectivity, and harmony. This primer is designed to work with you, rather than school you, or pretend to impart some ancient secret!

Believe it or not, you have all the tools you need to call upon the "secret," which is discovering and utilizing your power. You have a brain, spirit, and a hunger to know. More of what you have, you will hone. These teachings will provide you with rituals and alternatives to instant gratification. Along those lines, remember strong spell-work takes time. Perhaps some of us lack focus, direction, and in some cases, hope. Again, work with Wicca, and then watch and see. All you need to do is surrender to the wisdom inherent in you. What you can expect from these pages is a primer that will help you to help yourself. Even if you have been on the path for a while, and feel you are beyond the basics, this book offers you spell-work, guided visualizations, recipes, and information that can enhance your practice. The text is double-spaced to allow ample room for notes and to create your own dialog. Additionally, to aid your studies, Spirit Stones and a supplemental CD are available through the contact information on page 307.

You will find that when I give you work to complete, I tag it as "ritual" instead of an "exercise." Here's why: You are sacred and so is the work you do with your sacred body temple. The word ritual implies that the act done is one of reverence and one that will be repeated. The more often we repeat the act, the stronger the energy associated with it. By no means should your ritual work be inflexible or highly stylized. Simply think of these rituals as sacred ceremonies between you and the temple of self. You are free to substitute and adjust the work in any way that aids you in working toward your greatest good.

Because these teachings began as a diary, there are stories and musings, which I hope will color your journey. You will also find that I spell the word "magick" with a "ck." This is a stylization that I, and many others, used in the early 90s to set ritual magic apart from parlor magic and other forms. It's now a personal preference for me. The primer is designed to take you by the hand as *we* walk the path.

With that said, we are already at lesson # 1, which is patience. Remember, magick takes time. To rush is often to ruin. Welcome to the *Teachings of an Outlaw Witch.*

Chapter 1

Attunement

Millions of Americans suffer from Attention Deficit Disorder (ADD) and/or Attention Deficit Hyperactivity Disorder (ADHD), serious conditions that should be professionally monitored. However, for many of us the problem is not a medical one. Instead, our minds simply wander. It's this lack of focus, or absence of consciousness, that ultimately puts us in our own way. If your failure to focus isn't medically based, then let's take a look at how we can work toward centering both our focus and our energy.

What's that chatter, the voice that simply won't keep quiet? Crazy? Absolutely not. If you take a moment to sit with stillness, then you realize that unless you are completely focused on the stillness, there is a voice sounding in the back of your mind. That's ego chatter. We tend to keep a constant and often unconscious monologue in our heads. We may be diligently performing a task: cooking, working, driving. If we take a moment to be still, we realize that while cooking, we are replaying the day's events. While working, we may be engaging different scenarios about our situation. Driving is the most notorious act, because we may be planning what we'll do when we arrive at our destination, rather than focusing on the journey. The bottom line is that what we're doing does not have our full attention. So, the question becomes how to silence the voice, or at least keep it down to a dull roar. This ritual may serve as an answer.

Flame of Focus

Psychic Sit-ups

Meditation works as a tool of concentration and focus. It places you in a relaxed state of consciousness. This state promotes attunement to psychic signals and harmony with the collective unconscious. Skim the requirements to ensure you have the items needed. Then, take a moment to read the steps. They are easy to follow, but if you scan them first, your meditation will be seamless.

Remember to ensure you have what is needed before performing each ritual.

You will need:

♦ A quiet spot to meditate

♦ (1) White candle (small chime candles sold at most health and metaphysical shops are best).

The Ritual

Find a place where you won't be disturbed. Dim all the lights and draw the drapes so that you can work by the light of your candle. Sit comfortably. Take (3) deep, cleansing breaths, breathing in and exhaling through your nose. When you feel comfortable and grounded by the breaths, sit before the lit candle and focus on the flame. Watch the flame's movement. Does it sway or burn tall? Focus on the flame, but soften your gaze. After a few minutes, close your eyes. The image of the flame will remain on your inner lids.

CONCENTRATE on this inner image. **The object is to focus your thoughts and powers of visualization on the image of the flame for as long as possible.** When outer world thoughts and concerns intrude, conclude the ritual.

PRESCRIPTION: Repeat the ritual daily over the course of several weeks. Each time, work to extend the period of concentration. Keep a journal of your progress, noting the length of time you were able to hold the visualization.

Why We Focus

You have just completed your first ritual and are beginning your walk along the path that is Wicca. You may be wondering why a primer on Wicca begins with a ritual on visualization. The reason is that magick is all about directing intent. That means we focus our energies and intentions on a desired outcome. That's pretty difficult to do if we cannot first find the place of stillness. This ritual and the guided visualizations that you will find sprinkled throughout the primer are designed to allow you to seek and find the space of stillness.

She approached a fiery-haired Goddess. Her call, the call as old as time. When the student is ready, so the teacher shall appear. I found her. I found my calling.

Notes of a Priestess

Chapter 2

The Calling and The Wheel

Nearly twenty years ago, I found my teacher and my way into Wicca quite by accident. Our meeting was by chance, but it changed the course of my life. I learned a great deal from my High Priestess and incorporate much of her teachings into my work as a High Priestess. I am forever grateful to her for making Wicca and magick accessible. I will share with you the history as it was taught to me. This is by no means an in-depth study in the history of Wicca. It is your introduction, coven style. I have crafted an accurate accounting of the highlights of Wicca, in keeping with the oral tradition, so that you have a background for the energies and concepts you will be working with. See the bibliography for complete texts.

Wicca

Wicca is a specific sect or discipline of *The Craft*. Wiccans are considered pagans, because a pagan religion is any religion that predates Christianity, and/or one whose religion does not conform to the world's main religions, which are Judaism, the Muslim Faith, and Christianity. However, because Wicca is a specific religious sect with its own tenets, not all pagans are Wiccans.

As an oral tradition, there is no history of Wicca per se. Gerald Gardner is credited with bringing the current practice of Wicca to what we refer to as the New Age. What we practice is not the age-old practice of our ancestors; rather it is Gardner's and Anthropologist Margaret Murray's interpretation and enhancement of ancient customs, folklore, and traditions. Gardner claimed to have been initiated in 1939 by Dorothy Clutterbuck, a woman he considered a High Priestess. The coven from which Clutterbuck practiced was alleged to be descended from one of the "Nine Covens" founded by George Pickingill. Pickingill claimed his coven spanned eight centuries in an unbroken tradition. Gardner's interpretation of Pickingill's tradition and the Old Religion in general serve as a blueprint for what we call the modern practice of

Wicca.

In 1951 England, Gardner was instrumental in having the Witchcraft Act repealed, thus legalizing the practice of witchcraft. Though Gardner is credited with the blueprint, Alex Sanders is credited for popularizing Wicca and bringing it into the mainstream. Although there are many eclectic offshoots of the Wiccan practice, the two main sects in our time are the Gardnerian, of which my mother and grandmother coven are a part, and the Alexandrian Tradition, where the late Stewart Farrar and his wife Janet Farrar remain two of its most well known practitioners and authorities. Alex Sanders initiated the Farrars, who are the authors of *A Witches Bible Compleat*, a mainstay in any Wiccan's library.

There are many theories as to the origin of witchcraft. A commonly held perspective is that Wicca, and many aspects of witchcraft in general, evolved from animism—the belief that elements in nature, i.e., trees, earth, mountains, and the sky have souls or consciousness. As our understanding of our surroundings evolved, so too did our beliefs. Yet Wiccans, and most witches, continue to forge a bond with nature, viewing it as an aspect of The Divine.

What are the roots?

The modern meaning of Wicca refers to witchcraft and working in harmony with nature. Rosemary Ellen Guiley, author of *The Encyclopedia of Witches and Witchcraft,* asserts that the word Wicca may come from the Old English word "witta," meaning to bend. In many ways this is a logical assumption because witches bend or work with energies to realize their intent. In fact, we can define magick as the manifestation of change in the physical world. This is accomplished through directing our intent. In many ways magick and prayer are the same, because the core of each is directing one's intent toward a specific outcome.

Wicca is a nature-based religion. Its theistic roots center upon goddess represented as earth energy on the microcosm and moon energy on the cosmic or macrocosm. Wicca hinges upon the earth mother as goddess with reverence for nature and all life. Its key is balance. Does that mean the masculine element is excluded? *NO.* Wicca is monotheistic. It is a religion that embraces one deity and both its masculine and feminine aspects, realizing that all of nature is a delicate balance and nothing can occur without the balancing of the masculine and feminine principles.

The Nature of Wicca

Reverence for nature and life is illustrated through the interplay of Goddess and God. They dance the dance of creation. It is this dance that we, as Wiccans, honor. We do not simply exist on Earth. We are a part of the Earth, which is mother. The sun, which warms and gives life to the mother, is representative of God energy. Humans cannot exist without either and are a part of the cycle of creation. Wiccans do not worship the Earth, nor do we worship the Sun. Instead, we honor the creative forces and energies that each represents. The interplay of these energies symbolizes duality. You see, Wicca views deity as both immanent and transcendent. Immanence means deity doesn't exist outside of creation; deity is creation. It is nature. It is man, woman, and the world within which we exist. Transcendence means that deity also reaches though and beyond all levels of existence. Deity becomes universe, cosmos, all.

The Wiccan Rede

Before we embark on practice and the workings of magick, it's important to talk about the Wiccan Rede: ***And Ye Harm None, Do What***

Ye Will. This is the major tenet of Wicca and truly the core of how Wicca works. It sounds simple until you realize that your acts, your state of consciousness, must, to the best of your ability, reflect the greater good. There cannot be willful harm to you or others in thought, word, or deed. Essentially, it's about ethics. Work, speak, and practice from the Higher Self. Work in harmony with the spheres, nature, and all life toward the greatest good, realizing that there will be times when we have indeed consciously or unconsciously harmed someone or something. During these times, we must own the intentional and unintentional consequences of our acts. When we assess the nature of our actions, if we work with the awareness that we truly did the best we could with the tools and knowledge that we had at the time, then that is the first step toward ownership of consequences, both intentional and unintentional. However, our work does not stop there. If our realization is that we inflicted intentional harm when we were capable of doing otherwise, then we should and must work to right the situation. Even if restitution cannot be effected with the individual harmed, then our work should be toward "paying it forward" and working to change the negative consciousness and energy our deed released.

Secondly, we should understand the Three-fold Law of Karma. In some traditions it is seven-fold or more. For all the energy and intent we put forth, whether positive or negative, that same energy put forth returns to us in triplicate. Not in the same form, because that's not what karma is about. Karma isn't punishment, nor is it reward. It's simply the matching of like energies. Therefore, if we have done someone a kindness, positive energy will be reflected in our lives three-fold. Likewise, if we have acted unjustly, that energy will pass to us three-fold. The disbursement of energy isn't predicated on belief systems. In other words, if you say I don't believe in karma that doesn't mean that the energy you put out won't find its way back to you. Just as water finds its level, energies find their match in intensity and intent. As you work through the rituals in this book, choose your intent wisely and well. Work from your Higher Self, the spiritual place in you that is not based in greed, jealousy or destructiveness, rather it is the place of knowing that operates independent of ego for the sake of the greater good.

Lastly, understand that not all harm is physical or emotional. Before you embark on working with energies, particularly if you are drawn to the path of Wicca, realize that interfering with the freewill of another is HARM. We are all creatures of freewill. We are gifted with the abilities of rational thought and choice. It is not appropriate to work magick or bend energies in order to deprive another of his or her freewill.

The Wheel Of The Year

There's a song that's sometimes sung in ritual: *Turn, turn wheel of the year, season's change has brought us here, ever changing, always near, turning round and round.* This is one of my favorite songs, because it speaks of the cycle of life, of nature. Wiccans refer to this cycle as The Wheel of the Year. The wheel is the circle, which is complete within itself—infinite and timeless. It is the cycle of the seasons. It is nature, which is realized through each of us, as we move through life and ultimately death and rebirth. It is the heart of the Old Religion.

As the wheel of the year turns, we see life unfold in seasons, from the first buds of spring, to the withered branches of winter. We watch the moon's cycles and the tides. We look for imagery representative of the presence of The Lady and The Lord, and we find it in the shining moon and the rising sun. The moon, with its cycles and phases, is representative of Goddess energy. In contrast, the sun, with its brilliant rise and set, represents the cycle of God energy.

Why Moon and Sun?

The Goddess aspect, like the moon, resides over the changing tides in our lives. These tides are emotions, and in nature they are the embodiment of water, the spirit of the sea. Water is considered a feminine energy and an aspect of consciousness. Like both moon and sea, the Goddess shines bright, but possesses a darker side, that of crone energy. The Crone is the Lady of Magick. She is The Dark Mother who cuts the thread of life that we may be born again.

The God as consort to the Goddess is an equal aspect that lends balance. He is the bright and shining sun, promising growth and fertility. He is the twilight of the setting sun, which rests in darkness. As the Dark Lord, he is sacrifice. He has given of himself so that earth may thrive. Like the Crone, in this aspect, he is mystery and magick.

The Seasons – The Sabbats

If you already know the correspondences of the seasons and the sabbats, test your knowledge and draw a chart that includes the information that follows.

- The month

- The sabbat

- The date of the sabbat

- The energy the sabbat represents

- Lore associated with the sabbat

You can check your chart against the one provided at the end of this section.

There are eight sabbats/festivals that occur during the year. These sabbats reflect the changing tides of nature. In addition to the information on sabbats provided in this primer, Janet and Stewart Farrar's *A Witches Bible Compleat* provides detailed information on each sabbat, including The Witches New Year in October, specifically Samhain, pronounced Sow (like the "ow" in cow) -en, Oct 31st. This is largely because Wicca is a pagan/pre-Christian religion and is not predicated on the solar/Gregorian Calendar. Instead, Oct 31st represents the eve of the Celtic winter. This date is in opposition to May Eve or Beltane, which welcomes summer.

Samhain, October 31st

This is considered a major sabbat. Please note that major is not used in the sense of greater versus lesser, rather it means that cosmic energies run stronger during certain times as opposed to others. For instance, at Samhain, god energy prevails and The Lord will reign from Samhain to Beltane. Samhain is a time when the veil between the worlds is the thinnest. What this means is that there is little to interfere with contacting consciousness from the realm of those who have passed on. What's more, it is a time when psychic energy is high, which makes it ideal for scrying and other forms of intuitive contact. In times past, Samhain represented the final harvest. All crops had to be harvested and all fit livestock slaughtered so that life might be sustained for the coming barren months of winter. In a world that is no longer predominantly agricultural, Samhain represents a mental harvest. It is at this time that we take stock and reflect upon our accomplishments. We turn within and look to our spirit guides for direction. We commune with the past, while in the present, and ultimately we look to the future. Samhain represents a time without boundaries, a time of both productivity and preparation. Because it is a sabbat it is not a time of work, but rather one of celebration and reflection. In my coven, we often decorate our altar with squash and Indian corn, symbols of the final harvest. We also sprinkle fall leaves and burn mystical incense blended with mugwort to aid in scrying. In the Table of Correspondences, I provide a full listing of tools for the celebration of Samhain and for each of the eight sabbats. Advanced students, feel free to leap ahead.

December 21st Yule

Yule represents the Winter Solstice. It is the counterpart to the Summer Solstice known as Litha, and from a seasonal standpoint it is the shortest day of the year. When we view Yule from the mythical standpoint, a fascinating tale is spun. Here, the Holly King, also know as the Dark Lord, battles the Oak King, Lord of Light, for the favor of the Goddess. These two brothers come together. One must fall, one prevail. As the wheel turns, it is the Lord of Light who prevails. His victory signals the closing of winter, the dark time, and a move into the light. As weeks turn to months, the days grow progressively longer and warmer. The Goddess now walks the path with the Lord of Light. Together, they will bring growth and renewal to the land.

Yule is a fascinating sabbat, because mythical lore abounds. It is a time of death, birth, and renewal, a time when all aspects of the Goddess and the God are present. Consider for a moment, in the first tale, the Dark Lord is sacrificed so that the Lord of Light may reign and bring life to the land with The Lady. Another aspect to the sabbat of Yule is the coming of the Young Lord. The Goddess assumes the mother aspect and gives birth to the Young Lord. Because his birth heralds the reign of light, the maiden aspect of the Goddess also stands in attendance. Additionally, the dark time is dying; therefore, the crone aspect of the Goddess is in attendance as well. Here, we see the tri-fold Goddess at her height. She is Maiden, Mother, and Crone. Likewise, the God assumes three aspects. He is the Young Lord, birthed from the mother. He is the Lord of Light, who has battled his brother for control of the seasonal tides, and he is the Dark Lord, who relinquishes his reign.

When we celebrate Yule we honor this sabbat with a Yule Log, traditionally oak. Pinecones symbolize fertility and candles represent the three aspects of the Goddess: white for the Maiden, red for the Mother, and black for the Crone. We also light a green candle for the Young Lord. Rich and heady incense such as Frankincense and Myrrh are burned and excitement abounds. Look for the tree blessing ceremony in the Appendix. This ceremony is necessary for all who bring cut trees into their homes.

February 2nd Imbolc

Imbolc translates from the Irish oimelc, "ewe's milk." We think of it as representing pregnancy or "in the belly." For Wiccans it is the beginning of the winter thaw and a time to plan for planting the seeds of growth and renewal. The land remains frozen and hard. Light does not rule the sky, yet we see a softening as the sun's rays melt away the face of winter. My tradition, which is rooted in the Gardnerian Tradition, but has evolved into Celtic-eclectic, celebrates Imbolc as the time of Brigid, the Celtic Goddess of poetry and smith-craft. She represents inspiration and creativity. Therefore, it is at this time of the year that we give serious consideration to what we wish to reap in the months ahead. Whether Wiccan or not, this is an excellent time for planning, because you have recovered from the holidays, the year is new, and promise abounds. In celebration of Brigid we make corn dollies, because corn is symbolic of fertility and promise. We also light a fire in the cauldron. Into this cauldron we drop slips of paper. One slip of paper contains that which we wish to be shed of, and the second slip contains that which we wish to actualize. The former is dropped into the cauldron because fire is transformative. It is both a destructive and creative force. It purifies, cleanses, and sets the stage for renewal. We save the latter, what we wish to actualize, upon our altar. The cauldron ritual is one you may want to try in order to pave the path of your desires.

March 21st Ostara

Ostara is representative of the Vernal/Spring Equinox. Here, the powers of light and dark are in balance, yet light is on the winning side. The thaw is well underway and we see buds of promise bloom across the land. Ostara is a time of true fertility and creativity. The Lord of Light and The Lady of the Lake are young and playful. They hold the promise of life within their hands and close to their hearts. Our altar cloths are soft pastels with decorative eggs placed about. The egg symbolizes not only fertility, but its oval shape represents the complete cycle of life—beginning, middle, end, and 'round again. From the time of Imbolc until now, we planned and visualized what we wished to actualize. Now is the time to plant the seeds and to put our plans into motion. We work with vibrant fragrances, such as ylang-ylang, which are excellent for promoting balance. We work in the spirit of harmony, effecting balance in our personal and spiritual lives, so that our creative expanse is fertile.

May 1st Beltane

Beltane represents the sacred union or marriage between The Lady and The Lord, now Lady and Lord of the Green. This is the time of the Goddess and she reigns from Beltane to Samhain. Beltane is a sabbat filled with sensual energy. Our lives, our bodies, and our energy levels are ripe with promise. The seeds of our desires have been planted and now receive nurture from The Lady and Lord. The Maypole is symbolic of this fertile, sensual energy, with the pole penetrating the warm earth. A garland tops the pole, again a symbol of fertility as the lingam penetrates the circle, which is the circle of life. We dance, weaving the ribbons that hang from the maypole's lofty heights as promise for what we wish to actualize. The heady fragrance of amber fills the air, and at night we burn a Beltane fire. It is across this fire that we jump, our leap symbolic of personal and spiritual transformation.

June 21st Litha/Summer Solstice

On June 21st we celebrate the Lord of Light at his height, as the sun reaches its highest point in the sky. Also on this date, the Oak King and the Holly King meet once more in battle. Each brother vies for the hand of The Lady. At the close of the night the Holly King prevails, and we enter the time of the Dark Lord. In the comings days, the sun will

sink lower. The days shall grow shorter. We bid farewell to summer and

embrace the reign of the Dark Lord. Although some may find the term

"Dark Lord" ominous, rest assured, there is nothing ominous about this

aspect of the god. He tends to the children of earth and will ultimately

sacrifice himself at Lughnasadh, considered the first harvest. Yet, on this

day, joined with his lady, he is the God of the Green, while The Lady is

considered Lady of the Flowers. For this reason, Litha is a time of revelry

and celebration. It is a time to seek out the meadows and woods and

cull fresh herbs to fuel our magick. For those who are city bound, it's a

great time to visit an herbalist or aromatherapist to stock up on supplies

for blending our own incense and oils. See the Correspondences for the

Sabbats chart at the end of this section for ideas. And don't worry,

Chapter 6 is devoted to essential oil blends and herb work!

August 1st Lughnasadh (Loo-na-sa)

August 1st symbolizes the first harvest. In my tradition this is

known as Lughnasadh, in honor of the Celtic Sun God, Lugh. A master of

the arts and all crafts, Lugh sacrificed himself for the land, returning as a

sheaf of wheat. In relation to this myth, other names for this sabbat include Lammas and/or Loaf Mass. These terms relate to the fact that in times past, loaves of bread were baked from the grain of the first harvest and then blessed. Now, we celebrate the sabbat with breads such as wheat or cornbread. Apples and fruit adorn our celebration as well. We do this in honor of the god's sacrifice. Symbolically, the sabbat represents the fact that the fruits of our labor are now ripe for harvest. The planning and planting of Imbolc and Ostara, as well as the nurture gained at Beltane and Litha, have paved the way for the harvests to come.

September 21st Mabon/Autumn Equinox

Considered the Witches' Thanksgiving, Mabon celebrates the second harvest. Here we reap the bounty of the land. Our altars are decorated with cornucopias overflowing with fruits, corn, gourds, and rich grains. This sabbat signals the manifestation of our plans. It is also the time of the Autumn Equinox, where we see balance between the forces of light and dark, yet dark remains on the winning side. What this means is that we do not enter a time of action as we did during Ostara- The Spring Equinox- rather we enter a time of rest and reflection. As mentioned before, we now reap all that we have sown in seasons past.

We've just circled 'round the Wheel of the Year. At the end of this section, there are charts that will help you to coordinate tools, colors, and supplies for each of the eight sabbats. They will serve you well as you learn lessons in correspondences. Now, it's time to turn our attention to the traditional gathering time of the witch. The esbat.

Esbats

An esbat signifies the gathering of witches during the full moon. At this time we work magick, cast spells, and attend to coven duties if we are working as a group. We honor The Lady and The Lord through our ritual work. During the appropriate time of the year, initiations, granting of degrees, and other ritual tasks are also performed on the night of the full moon. In months with a "Blue Moon," the second full moon in a month, we may meet twice; hence there are thirteen moons to the cycle of our year.

The Reflective Pool

Full Moon Visualization

Working with the moon's energy is an excellent way to learn how to work with the *Table of Correspondence*. By simply using this ritual, you can learn how to work with and draw in the energy that corresponds to each month's full moon. Read the steps. They are bulleted and easy to follow. If you scan them first, your meditation will be seamless. **Remember to ensure you have what is needed before performing each ritual.**

You will need:

(1) Glass or Crystal bowl

(1) 8-16 oz. bottle of filtered or spring water to fill the bowl

Directions:

On the night of the full moon, find a safe and quiet place where you won't be disturbed. Although best performed outside, this ritual can be done inside while gazing at the full moon, modify accordingly.

◆ Sit beneath the full moon.

◆ Place the bowl of water to the side.

◆ Allow the moonlight to shine upon the water's surface.

◆ Take (3) deep cleansing breaths. As you inhale, draw in positive, silver-light energy, as if you were drawing it down from the moon.

◆ Exhale through your mouth and see yourself exhale any grey negativity or heaviness.

♦ Next, gaze into the bowl. Allow your thoughts to reflect upon all of the positive energy that has filtered into your life. Imagine the positive moments reflected upon the water's surface. If negativity crosses your thoughts, offer the bowl toward the moonlight and envision the light of the moon casting away dark, negative energy.

♦ Drink the water from the bowl and imagine the silver moonlight working through your veins, infusing you with The Goddess's guiding light and positive energy. Allow yourself to internalize this energy.

♦ Take several moments to quietly reflect upon the good in your life. Sip from the bowl and feel the cleansing energy flow through you. Take as much time as you need to finish the water, drinking in healing moments and emotions.

♦ In closing, offer a prayer of thanks to The Goddess. *Blessed be.*

End of Chapter Charts and Correspondences

The Wheel of The Year

Season	Spring	Summer	Fall	Winter
Cycle	Birth	Life	Aged	Death/Rebirth
Direction	East	South	West	North
Element	Air	Fire	Water	Earth
Sabbats	Ostara, Beltane	Litha, Lughnasadh	Mabon Samhain	Yule, Imbolc

Sabbats are the Holy Days of Wicca

Esbats are Recognition of Each Full Moon

Correspondences for the Sabbats

Sabbat	Associated Colors	Associated Tools	Associated Herbs/Scents
Samhain	Orange, black	Gourds, cauldrons, corn, scrying mirrors, apples, brooms	Cinnamon, dragon's blood(R), mugwort**, (P) sage (W), star anise**(P)
Yule	Green, red, white, black, silver, gold	Oak (Yule log) pine cones, holly, mistletoe	Cedar, frankincense, myrrh, pine, rosemary (M),
Imbolc	White, gold	Solar wheels, corn dollies, chakra stones	Chamomile, copal(R), jasmine* lilly, vervain
Ostara	All pastels especially yellow, pink, green	Eggs, flowers, symbols of fertility	Bergamot, lavender, lemongrass, neroli, pennyroyal
Beltane	Rich reds, greens, silver, gold	Maypole, chalice, garlands, cauldron,	amber, rose, rose geranium, saffron** vanilla
Litha	Yellows, reds	Herbs, fruits, sunflowers, sweets for fairies	Cinquefoil**, jasmine, orange blossom, rosemary, ylang, ylang

Correspondence for the Sabbats (cont.)

Lughnasadh	Orange, yellow, gold	Bread, grains, fall fruits, corn, wheat,	Allspice**, clary sage, clove, ginger, nutmeg
Mabon	Orange, yellow, gold, red	Corn, squash, bread, grains,	Patchouli, vetivert, vervain, valerian** yerba santa**,

Legend: W = Wisdom P = Psychic Energy M = Magickal Energy R = Primarily a resin

* All are great for peace and spirituality

** Most easily acquired in herb form

Remember, candles in the corresponding colors are always recommended for each sabbat. Silver and gold candles can be used to represent Goddess and God energy respectively.

This table is by no means all inclusive. I have chosen scents/herbs that are relatively easy to come by and whose properties and associations correspond well to the given sabbat. Feel free to add or substitute as it suits you.

The crystal wand shone, clear-cut in its beauty. She held it in her hands amazed by the heft, the power. She stood as if spellbound. Then, the voice of her teacher, her priestess, echoed in the stillness. "You are the maker of the magick." With care she returned the wand to its case and then set about her lessons.

Notes of a Priestess

Chapter 3

Tools of the Witch

Your mind is the greatest tool you possess as a witch. This chapter focuses on meditations to help you hone your skills and offers traditional tools that aid in the work of the witch. When we are new to The Craft, one of the most exciting aspects is gathering magickal tools. Before we rush off to make or purchase the means of our magick, let's take stock in what we have—the power of our minds.

Magick is the result of directing our intent. We accomplish feats of magick through the ability to visualize our goal and then direct our energy toward that means. Remember *The Flame of Focus?* That was our first psychic sit-up. Now it's time for another.

The Memory Stone

Psychic Sit-ups

Select a tumbled stone. Because amethyst possesses both psychic and visionary energies, I recommend it. However, any tumbled stone you choose will work.

You will need:

♦ A quiet spot to work. Your altar or your personal power spot are excellent choices.

♦ The tumbled stone

♦ (1) White candle

Directions:

Study the stone. Note the color(s) and shading. Note the contours, ridges, and imperfections. Feel the shape of the stone in your hands. Take a mental picture of all that you see and feel. Holding a clear picture of the stone, close your eyes and recreate it in your mind's eye. Construct it through the memory of touch, texture, and color until you can visualize the very stone you hold.

Repeat this ritual 2-3 times a week, until you can train your mind to create accurate images.

Use the space provided to record any notes or observations.

| |
| |
| |
| |
| |
| |

The preceding ritual promotes discipline in the area of visualization and is excellent for focusing intent and mental energy. Use it to quiet the mental back-talk that may run through your mind. In order to manifest your desires, you must be able to visualize them.

Directing and focusing intent works hand in hand with visualization. In truth, magick cannot function effectively without the practitioner taking the time to hone these skills. Once we take a look at prayer and intent, we will be ready to examine the use of tools that can aid our focus. Even if you feel inclined to skip ahead, I encourage you to try your hand at this next ritual. If nothing else, it can surely deepen your practice.

In the work that follows, we will use the basics of prayer to understand intent. Before you delve into magickal workings and manifesting your desires, you must be sure of your intent. What is intent? *It is the directing of our energies toward manifestation of desire.* Working magick is not the subject of this ritual, nor this particular lesson. Here are points to consider prior to embarking on any magickal or mundane endeavor:

◆ Does what you wish to manifest work toward the greater good?

◆ Is it for the self or self-serving? These are two very different concepts. For example, bringing love into one's is a fine intent and much magick has been worked in this regard. To make a specific person love you becomes self-serving and works against the greater good, not to mention that individual's free will.

Prayer and Intent

You will need:

◆ Pen or Pencil

◆ A Journal, notebook or parchment paper

Directions:

Write a prayer. It is symbolic of your intent. Remember, that which we pray for represents the directing of our intent toward god/goddess in an effort to help in manifesting our desire. Consider writing the Goddess a prayer for guidance in your endeavors. Below is an example.

Gracious Goddess, please bless me and guide me as I work toward manifesting my desires. Grant me the wisdom and the will to make the choices that are best for my and the greatest good.

To the God aspect, write a prayer of thanks for his protection and nurture of both you and The Lady. You will find an example below.

Gracious God, thank you for your guidance, protection, and nurture. Ever do I seek to direct my energies that they may be a reflection of your work—as above, so below.

Keep your prayer simple, one that you can easily memorize and repeat to connect you to divine energy. The assignment asks that you write two prayers in order to fortify your intent. However, feel free to direct your prayers to The Lady and The Lord collectively. Either way, you will ultimately connect to the greater consciousness.

Workspace: Use the space provided to draft your ideas. You can then transfer the final product to your journal or **Book of Shadows**, which is **a personal, written record of your spells, rituals, and all magickal endeavors.**

We have seen that the mind is the greatest magickal tool at our disposal. However, let's work now to integrate what we have learned. We will start with a guided visualization and learn how it can lead us to finding the magickal tools that we need in the physical world. Using the supplemental CD, go to the *Forest Path* meditation. Otherwise, use the printed version for the visualization and the assignment that follows.

The Forest Path

Guided Visualization

See yourself on a forest path. The light of the full moon guides you, while a carpet of pine needles crunches lightly beneath your feet. Inhale. Breathe in the crisp night air, hints of jasmine and lavender wafting upon the breeze. As you gaze up at the silvery light of the moon, your head and heart fill with appreciation and wonder.

The winding path leads you to a cottage just at the forest's edge. A trail of smoke rises from the chimney and creates a gossamer veil in the moonlight. The flame of a candle lights the cottage window. Star jasmine and roses weave along a trellis near the door. You approach. The wooden door is solid. You trace your fingertips along the magickal symbols etched into its surface. Upon touching the door, it opens. A

dulcet voice calls to you. She has been waiting. There is a familiarity to

her words, the sound of her voice. You step inside...

In the space provided, allow your intuition and imagination to

describe in detail who and what you see.

What does the cottage look like?

What is The Lady doing?

What do you talk about?

What does she tell you?

What gift does she give, and what gift do you leave?

***

This visualization is designed to allow the imagination to flourish. Perhaps you delved deeply and had a lengthy conversation with The Lady. Perhaps you imagined the types of tools you would require in your magickal practice and envisioned them within her cottage. Regardless of what you envisioned, imagination and visualization are wonderful gifts. Both will help you to discover and focus your intent, and they will serve you well as you work with the energies of the tools of The Craft.

Why Use Tools at All?

Tools are used to aid witches in spell-work and magick. I will never forget the time I was to cast circle for guests and elders of my mother coven. I had forgotten my wand and was in an absolute panic. That's when the crone of my mother coven pulled me aside and reminded me of one of my earliest lessons. *The magick resides within.*

She pointed out, no pun intended, that my index finger could serve as a fitting wand. I took her advice, and a deep breath, relaxed, and the circle flowed wonderfully.

"The magick resides within." The tools of the witch are tools of

focus. They can be beautiful and striking to behold, yet they do not

create the magick. A skilled practitioner can as easily direct the energy

through the vessel of her/his body. Remember this as we explore the

contents of the witches' toolbox.

Basic Tools of the Witch

I have broken down the information to represent the traditional

symbols and tools of the Goddess, as well as the basic tools found on a

Wiccan altar. Notice that there are two columns. The information to the

left represents those tools that are considered feminine; hence the left

is the side of the Goddess. Correspondingly, those symbols and tools

considered masculine are on the right, which is representative of the

side of the God.

Sample Altar Setup

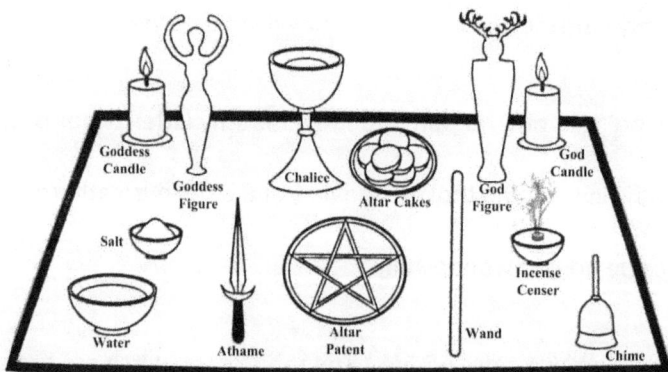

God and Goddess Representation

Traditional Symbols for the Goddess	Traditional Symbols for the God
The moon	The sun
A crescent	A horn (antlers*)
A bowl	The maypole
Flowers	Oak
Cultural goddess figurines and statues	Cultural god figurines and statues
*Naturally shed antlers. We do not endorse hunting for sport.	

The Basics of A Wiccan Altar

Goddess Symbol/Figure	God Symbol/Figure
Pentacle	Censer for charcoal
Container/dish for sea salt	Dish for incense
Dish for water	Wand
Flowers or greenery (always fresh)	Sword
Athame (black handled knife)*	Matches
Chalice	Broom
Plate for altar cakes	Chime
Cauldron	Boline (white handled knife)

*As this is the practitioner's tool, it is the sex of the practitioner.

Use the space provided to design your altar set-up

The Breakdown

Tool	Masculine	Feminine	Element	Purpose
Pentacle	Yes, (symbol of humanity as well)	Yes	Earth	To ground, cleanse, and charge tools
Athame	Yes, represents the element of air	Yes, the tool of the Goddess	Air	Can be used to cut circle and direct energy/ cannot be used to cut anything physical
Boline	Same as above	Same as above	Air	To cut herbs and other ritual items
Chalice	No	Yes, symbolic of the womb	Water	To hold ritual beverages, also used for The Great Rite
Wand	Yes	No	Fire	To direct energy and charge circle and other ritual items
Sword	Yes	No	Air	To cut circle, and for other sacred rites
Broom	Yes, phallic	Yes, feminine	Air	To clear energy Also used in "flying rites"

The Breakdown (cont.)

Chime	Yes	No	Air	To call circle and change consciousness
Cauldron	No	Yes, symbolic of the womb	Water	To scry, magickal rites, and is symbolic of transformation
Flowers	No	Yes	Earth	Homage to the deities
Salt	No	Yes	Earth	Blend with spring water to cleanse and charge
Water	No	Yes	Water	To cleanse and charge
Incense	Yes	No	Air	Blend with charcoal to cleanse and charge

I stand upon the shore, warm sand beneath my feet, the kiss of sunlight against my cheek, cloaked only by the embrace of the wind. The call, age old, coaxes me—though some might hear only the gentle lap of waves. I cross the line where the ocean meets the land and feel Yemaya's caress. Goddess, guide me. Goddess, bathe me in your love. In this sacred space, I am home. The gentle touch of Yemaya washes me clean.

My encounter with Yemaya—Afro-Caribbean Goddess of the Sea

Notes of a Priestess

Chapter 4

Creating Sacred Space

In order to work magick effectively, it is important to create an environment conducive to the endeavor. Sacred space must exist both within and without. Let's ease into the idea with a guided visualization. Use the Crystal Pool visualization on the supplemental CD, or use the printed version. Enjoy!

The Crystal Pool Visualization

Breathe deeply. As you inhale, imagine a crystal river of breath flowing through your body, cleansing and refreshing you. This crystal river fills you with calm. As you exhale, the river washes away fatigue

Exhale and release. Inhale once more, breathing in cool, calm energy. With each exhale, release.

Now, see yourself at the mouth of a cave. The cave walls are soft pink, the color of Rose Quartz. A full moon shines down upon you. The air is still. You are alone, safe. You reach for a lighted torch at the mouth of the cave and then enter. You wind a path down, while torchlight plays against the rose-pink coloring of the walls and a warming glow envelops you.

As you walk, you place a marker to help you remember your way back. Stop and study the cave. Take care as you place your marker, then move on. Soon, you reach the bottom of the path to stand before a sparkling underground pool. The water is clear and blue, with white lotus flowers floating on the surface. You strip off your clothes and then enter the water. It is softly fragranced with the scent of sandalwood and vanilla. It washes warm against your skin, cleansing and refreshing you.

As you bathe, you catch your reflection and see the signs of fatigue, worry, stress, and negativity wash from your body, sliding down your skin and dissipating into the crystal pool.

You are cleansed and refreshed. You step from the pool. Soft towels await you. Dry yourself.

Beside the towels rests a blue bottle. You reach for it and mist yourself with a light, lavender fragrance. Your energy now balanced, you dress, feeling calm and refreshed.

You reach for your torch, and wind your way back. Find your marker. It will guide you to the door of the cave. With every step, the soft, pink glow of the walls envelops and caresses you. Your steps are slow, your body relaxed. When you are ready, find your way to the doorway of the cave. Replace the torch, so that it will await you the next time. Step through the door, and find your way back to us here.

Cleansing the Temple: Why This Type of Visualization is Important.

1. Appropriate mindset: You and your intent must be clean and clear of negativity. Your mind and body must be receptive to positive energy.

2. Grounding: Without connection to earth and deity, we cannot create magick.

3. Guided intent: You need to see what you wish to actualize and to see yourself as already having that which you desire.

***

The clearing and cleansing of both mental and physical space are important aspects of ritual, yet that is only the beginning. The environment in which we work must be prepared as well. To that effect, nature provides us with a bounty of supplies. Outlined are some of the techniques and tools available and how they can be used to make your home and environment safe and sacred.

Planting:

Many witches plant **rosemary** near their front doors and in their gardens for protection. If you live in an apartment, condominium, or have limited space a potted rosemary plant works fine. Rosemary is a wonderful addition to your ritual tool chest, because the herb can be used for cooking and magickal recipes, too.

Lavender, a masculine herb ruled by Mercury, god of war, works for both purification and protection. Additionally, both French and English lavender possess a wonderful smell. A lavender bush near your front door offers protection. By rubbing your hands on the leaves and flowers, and then rubbing your clothing, you can purify yourself before entering your home. This is yet another plant that complements limited space, as you can buy a small, potted lavender plant. What's more, you will find it indispensable in your magickal repertoire, because many

spells and rituals call for its use.

Lastly, **Red Ornamental Peppers** also offer protection and are a

decorative addition to your garden or windowsill.

On the Spot Protection

In many traditions, salt plays an important role in protection. Sea

salt, in particular, cleanses and purifies well. A modified ritual drawn

from my Vodou heritage is to sprinkle sea salt across the front entrance

of your home. Those with ill intent will be remiss to cross your

threshold. If you want to strengthen this protective ritual, then create a

mixture that is (3) parts **vervain herb** to (1) part sea salt. Vervain wards

off/ drives away evil spirits. Sprinkle the mixture around the perimeter

of your property and in the corners of your home.

Cleansing Indoor Spaces:

White sage is highly desirable for cleansing and purifying sacred

space. You can burn it by the leaf or bundle. The process is called

smudging. Here's how it's done:

◆   Light the leaves. Ensure that you hold them in a heat resistant container. Censors or abalone shells work well.

♦ Begin in the east and work clockwise (deosil). If you plan to smudge your entire home, begin in the east, walking and working clockwise throughout. If your house is more than one story, begin on the lower floor, always in the east.

♦ As you clear the area, make sure you fill the void with clean intent. While smudging, you may want to say something to this effect: "I cleanse this space with love and fill it with blessings from above."

♦ Use a white feather to fan the smoke.

Sacred Space Spritzers:

1. A blend of sea salt and spring water is great for cleansing small or large spaces. Use **1 teaspoon of salt** to **1 cup of spring water.** You can use a white feather or a sage wand as an aspergillum and simply sprinkle the blend throughout the house and/or area that requires cleansing. Note: because the quality of tap water varies between regions, I often recommend distilled or spring water. However, it is fine to use the water that you find suitable and available.

2. **Lavender Aura Mists** are great for cleansing, protecting, and

purifying both your space and you. Start with **3 to 9 drops of Lavender essential oil to 1 cup of distilled water.** Lavender is a strong scent; adjust the amount of oil used to suit your taste. Always shake well before application, as oil and water separate. You can mist yourself, the space, and/or any instruments that you wish to clean. If washing your magickal tools, ensure that you dry them well.

3. Another great way to cleanse your tools is to use the sea salt and spring water blend. Add **3 pinches of sea salt** to a small dish of **spring water**, and then light a white candle. Sprinkle the blend over the tools, wipe them down, and then dry them. Next, you will pass them through or over the flame of the white candle. Then, breathe your intent upon them. This is a modified version of the Wiccan cleansing and charging of tools, reinforcing the infusion of energy into the elements with which you work.

Casting a Pagan Circle

Casting a *Formal Wiccan Circle* is a part of the *Wiccan Mysteries*, and not the subject of this chapter. However, there are times when we need to create a sacred circle to contain our magickal work. *Pagan Circle* is a means of creating a safe working space. Like the formal circle, it adheres to strict rules. Unless directed to do so during a sabbat, or for specific reasons given by a High Priestess or High Priest, we always move clockwise (deosil) in our sacred space. Counterclockwise movement, (widdershins), serves the purpose of unwinding energy and is rarely used. Pagan circle works well for meditation and manifestation work as well as ritual. I recommend that you always keep a sage bundle on hand. It is an intrinsic part of your magickal repertoire. And although I will teach variations on creating a sacred circle in upcoming chapters, the pagan circle can work as your mainstay.

You will need:

♦ (1) White sage bundle

♦ Frankincense and Myrrh resin with charcoal, or incense sticks

♦ An abalone shell or ash catcher

♦ (1) Small, white working candle

♦ (1) White feather (optional)

Directions:

♦ Determine where you would like to create your sacred circle. Because this is your personal work, the perimeter of the circle can be quite small. As you cleanse the space, see your energy extending beyond the confines of the circle.

♦ Light the sage bundle. If you have a white feather, you may use it to fan the smoke.

♦ Beginning in the east, walk in a clockwise direction. Hold the bundle low, (allow your arm to extend to the height of your knee), and fan the smoke in an outward, sweeping motion. As you walk with the sage, state: "With fire and air, breath and life, I clear this space of impurities and strife."

♦ Return to your starting point in the east. Begin your circle again. Hold your arm out at shoulder level, and continue to fan the smoke in an outward, sweeping motion. Repeat, "With fire and air, breath and life, I clear this space of any impurities and strife."

♦ Return once more to your starting point in the east. When you walk the circle this time, raise your arm and fan the smoke up toward the ceiling. Once more state, "With fire and air, breath and life, I clear this space of any impurities or strife." Once you have completed the circle, extinguish the sage. Return to your altar, and then light the charcoal holding frankincense and myrrh resin, or incense stick.

♦ Beginning in the east, you will once more walk the circle three times. Each time you stand in the east state: "With fire and air,

breath and life, I fill this circle with blessings and light."

♦ You may leave the incense burning. Next, light your white candle,

speak your intent, and begin work in your circle.

Bright Blessings

Cloaked in white The Lady walks the circle, a chalice filled with sea salt and spring water in hand. Behind her the maiden holds a censer. Her voice strong and sure, The Lady chants, "with earth and water I do charge thee." The chalice raised, she sprinkles water about the circle. "With Fire and Air I do charge thee." She exchanges the chalice for the censer as aromatic smoke circles. Green and blue flashes capture my attention. Red and green lights spark my imagination. Feel the energy pulse—the smoke spin. With these words, let the magick begin.

Notes of a Priestess

Chapter 5

Elements and Elementals

Our allies in magickal work are the elements and elementals. These are terms you will hear throughout your walk along the path. You will work with the elements, which are the energies, and with their corresponding elementals, the mythical beings inherent in each element. First, let's talk about the elements. I will name them in the order in which Wiccans begin circle. We start with the **East.** The element is **Air**. We then move clockwise to the **South.** The element is **Fire.** From there we move to the **West,** where the element is **Water,** and then to the **North.** The element is **Earth.** Within this chapter you will find a handy chart for reference.

Each element has a corresponding elemental ruler and totem animal associated with it. In my tradition we call upon the following:

In the east, the elemental ruler is Paralda. He is the ruler of the sylphs, winged, fairy-like beings, and all creatures of air. Think of eagles, hawks, owls, and other winged beings as under his watch.

In the south we call upon Djinn, the powerful elemental ruler of fire. Salamanders and power animals are under his domain. Salamanders, because it was believed they could pass through fire without harm. Power animals are animals such as the mythic phoenix and dragon, as well as lions, horses, tigers, and snakes.

The domain of the west and water belongs to Niksa. As the elemental ruler, Niksa commands undines, similar to mer-people, and all creatures of water. Fish, whales, dolphins, and tortoises fall under Niksa's reign.

In the north, Gob is the elemental ruler of earth. He governs gnomes and creatures of land. Consider deer, squirrels, cattle, and all of earth's creatures a part of Gob's domain. As witches, we must know the elementals because they are the guardians of the sacred circle.

Guardians

The four cardinal directions comprise the (4) watchtowers in Wiccan and most pagan circles. The watchtowers are considered the protectors of sacred space. Their corresponding elementals are the guardians. In circle, we call upon the elementals or guardians to offer protection and to aid us in our magickal work. After all, magick is working with elements in order to manifest physically. However, let me interject a note of caution: when I say, "call upon," this means that we respectfully ask/invite their presence. We never command. The elements are not mortal, nor are their corresponding elementals. Neither falls under anyone's command. They are independent, immortal energies that should be accorded the utmost respect. Think of the many tragedies that have occurred when man seeks to conquer or place himself above nature.

In a Wiccan circle, we place candles at each of the four quarters to honor the elements. We will talk about the corresponding colors a bit later in the chapter. We then call upon the elementals or guardians of each quarter to endeavor their assistance. This is known as a **"Quarter call,"** and serves as our invitation. Though many pagan primers and books provide quarter calls, the best are those you write for yourself. The calls require an envisioning of the element, its corresponding color, and the elementals associated with each quarter. They should also include an outline of the purpose for which the quarters are called. Don't worry; it's not as daunting as it may appear. We will have the opportunity to see how everything fits together.

Now, take a look at the elements as teachers. Once more, begin in the east. Think fast! Who is the elemental ruler of the east? If you answered Paralda, you are absolutely right. What about the elementals? Sylphs and winged beings? Right again.

A great deal can be learned from the Eastern Quarter. More will be discussed in this chapter, and you will also find a Table of Correspondences for quick reference. We know the elemental ruler, Paralda, and the elementals under his watch. In addition to this, you can also regard the energy of the Eastern Quarter as that of "beginnings." Think in terms of fresh starts and new opportunities. Because the east is associated with the element of air, you may also relate this quarter to the intellect. If you sense a pattern of layering correspondences, you are correct. Each quarter possesses elemental rulers and elementals along with its distinct energies. And remember, I mentioned there are color correspondences associated with each quarter as well. The color correspondence for the **east** is **yellow**. The color relates directly to the time correspondence, which is dawn, and the time of year, which is spring.

If dedicating a space in your house to the Eastern Quarter interests you, consider draping a yellow cloth over a small table and decorating it with feathers and other symbols of air. *Caution: harm none. If you intend to find feathers for yourself, choose those that are naturally shed by the birds, or ensure that you purchase them from places that are sensitive to animal rights.* Pictures of winged beings or animal totem cards representing birds are a nice touch, too. Place the table in the east. Because the Eastern Quarter represents the element of air, you may include incense, sage, and magickal tools such as swords and/or athames. For a lasting and fragrant touch, fill a decorative ceramic dish with dried lavender, an herb that is most magickal and happens to be ruled by air!

The energy of the Southern Quarter is filled with passion, life, and power. It is the seat of creative flow. We know that the element is fire and we have discussed Djinn and the power animals. As you may have

guessed, the color correspondence for the **south** is **red**. The time is

noon and the time of year is summer. Knowing these correspondences,

begin a list of ways you might honor the Southern Quarter in your home

or on your altar. I have provided you with a workspace and example. In

fact, you can copy the list and use it as a worksheet for each of the

quarters.

Sample

Element	Attributes	Corresponding Items	Purpose/Energy
Fire	Life, passion, creativity	Candles, basil, cinnamon, clove, wands	To honor creativity in my life

Your Worksheet

Element	Attributes	Corresponding Items	Purpose/Energy

As you work with the correspondences, extend the reach of your imagination and think of ways to introduce some of the attributes of the Southern Quarter into your calls. For what reason might you call on mighty Djinn and the elementals of the south? Can you decorate your altar with red stones such as red jasper and still honor the south? Of course you can. You are working with the color correspondence as well as the natural property of the stone. The healing properties of the stone include aiding circulation and increasing energy and stamina.

The element of water speaks to our emotions and consciousness. Its energy is that of flow and feeling. We know that Niksa serves as elemental ruler of undines and other water creatures. As we layer the correspondences, it makes sense that the color is **blue** and the time of day, twilight, because the sun sets in the **west**. Additionally, fall would be the logical choice for the season, since fall is also the twilight of the year. Working with the energy of the Western Quarter affords us the opportunity to raise our consciousness and tap into hidden or long buried emotions. Imagine creating sacred space in the Western Quarter of your home. What would you include? For what reason, whether magickally or personally, might you call upon the elementals of the west?

Blue has long been recognized as a soothing and healing color. Perhaps you envision a corner lit with blue candles, or a shelf housing a small aquarium or fish bowl. How about an eclectic mix of seashells and pictures of loved ones upon a table draped with a velvety blue cloth?

There are countless blue stones, all with their own healing properties that can cover the surface of your sacred space. You are limited only by the boundaries of your imagination, so break down the borders and call upon the Western Quarter to aid you in healing, raising consciousness, and tapping into your emotions.

As we move around the circle, we come to the Northern Quarter. We are familiar with Gob and the myriad earth creatures of the realm. In my tradition, the Northern Quarter is also considered home to the Goddess or Mother. Therefore, the energy of the **north** is that of grounding and nurture. **Green** seems the logical color for this quarter, since it represents the green earth. The time associated with this quarter is midnight. Just as midnight is the dark time, it makes sense that the season for the north is winter, often considered the dark time of the year, because the days are shorter.

Many Wiccans place their altars in the northeast, because they are honoring the Goddess and the dawning energy of the Eastern Quarter. It is a wonderful idea to do so with your personal altar, and/or to create sacred space in the northeast corner of your home. Beautiful flowering or vine plants are a welcome addition, or perhaps a terrarium. You can make it as simple or as complex as you like. If you favor stones, what about an amethyst cathedral, or a sand or rock garden? If you are short on space, your favorite plant, stone, or even a picture of your pet will do. We have a beautiful pentacle wind chime in our home that serves as a constant reminder of the elements and the blessings of The Lady and The Lord. Some Wiccans leave daily offerings as token and reminder. The point is, you can choose one space in your home for an altar and recognize all elements upon it, or you can choose to honor the elements around your home. You really don't have to designate any particular area. By simply having representations of the elements in your home, you honor them. Recognizing their power and majesty is the first step in aligning and working with the elements and elementals.

The fifth element is Spirit, the soul of our being. We consider it the center. The color is black, for black is the absorption of all color. Black is considered the void before creation and The All. The time and season for Spirit is all time and all seasons. Therefore, spirit operates outside of traditional boundaries. It is governed by The Lady and The Lord—The All.

The Elemental Table of Correspondences

Element	Elemental	Ruler	Direction	Color
Air	Sylphs, fairies, winged creatures	Paralda	East	Yellow
Fire	Power animals	Djinn	South	Red
Water	Undines, water beings	Niksa	West	Blue
Earth	Gnomes, earthly creatures	Gob	North	Green

The Elemental Table of Correspondences (Supplemental)

Element	Time	Time of year	Keyword
Air	Dawn	Spring	Communication
Fire	Noon	Summer	Transformation
Water	Twilight	Fall	Flow
Earth	Midnight	Winter	Grounding

Ancient Celtic Correspondences

Direction	Color	Time
East	Red	Sunrise
South	White	High Noon
West	Blue	Twilight
North	Black	Midnight

You will note that I have included the ancient Celtic correspondences for the quarters as adapted from author D.J. Conway's *Celtic Magic.* Although my coven is Celtic-eclectic, we honor the traditional colors as outlined in the correspondence chart. However, it is always nice to know your heritage. If you would like to learn more about the Celtic tradition and add to your knowledge and practice, I strongly recommend Ms. Conway's *Celtic Magic.*

The Elements as Teachers

Were we to view the elements as teachers, each would possess a keyword. In this section, we will discover the keywords for each element. At the end of the chapter, there are assignments to help us integrate the teachings of the elements. Let's begin with air. Its keyword is **communication.** Our lessons become those of focus and breath, as well as clarity of thought and speech.

With fire as our teacher, **transformation** is the keyword, and our lesson is inspiration and the creative spark. Fire also fuels our passions. All of this is energy we can use to transform our lives.

For water, the keyword is **flow**. The element of water governs our deeper sense of consciousness and our emotions. When working with water, we seek fluidity in our lives. We learn flow. If you think about the nature of water, like earth, it is infinitely patient. It created the Grand Canyon, and it can wear a boulder down to a grain of sand.

Earth. Not surprisingly, the keyword is **grounding.** As we mentioned earlier, earth promotes patience. Anyone who has ever gardened knows the calming nature of earth. You can truly work your stress and concerns right into the earth.

Assignments

In the section that follows, you will find practical assignments for working with each of the elements. Those for air and fire are lengthy, those for water and earth, less so. This in no way reflects the importance placed on the elements, rather it provides a variety of approaches and accessible methods to familiarize yourself with each element. At the close of each activity is a *Merry Meet the Elements: Quick Picks Lesson*, so that you can put your skills to practice. Have Fun!

Air: The Magick of Breath

The Cleansing Breath

Sit comfortably, either on the floor, using a meditation cushion if you need to, or in a chair with your feet planted firmly on the ground, keeping your back straight.

♦ As you inhale through your nose, imagine that you are drawing breath from the root of your being. Allow the side ribs to expand slowly. Draw in the breath as though you were sipping the air through a straw. Feel the chest expand like a bellows. Allow the breath to fill the top of your head.

♦ When you exhale, do so through the nose. Allow the breath to flow out of you, from the top of your head, all the way down to your root. Imagine that you are a bellows and the air is being expelled from your body. Exhale completely. Repeat this process three times.

Alternate Nostril Breathing

♦ Read the instructions first. Learn the rhythm, and then give it a go. Do a complete cycle of (3) breaths.

♦ Use your **thumb** and **third finger only**. Press your **thumb** against your **right nostril**, and then **inhale through your left**. Take the same type of deep breath that you learned in the cleansing breath technique. Inhale from the root of your being. When you have reached the extent of your inhale, press your **third finger against your left nostril** and **exhale through your right nostril.**

♦ When you are ready to inhale, **keep your third finger pressed against your left nostril, and inhale through your right nostril.** You will **exhale through the left.** Then, inhale through the left, as you did to start, alternating the breath.

♦ It takes a moment to get the rhythm. Once you have it, deepen your breaths. Note how you felt before and after the breathing activity. You can begin with the assignment below.

Connecting Breath and Emotions

♦ Complete the sentence in the box. Try not to make it more than

one sentence, but compete the statement with more than one

word.

I feel....

Did you find this assignment easy to accomplish? Or, was it

challenging to succinctly state your feelings? The element of air

coordinates with our ability to communicate effectively in

thought, written, and oral communication. Often, deep breaths prior to composing a thought aid in the flow of ideas and how we express them.

The preceding activities are designed to help us focus on breathing and communication techniques. Many yogis and teachers of **Prana**—**vital breath**—will confirm that when people breathe deeply and slowly at an audible level, it produces a calming effect on those around them. From now on, at least twice a day, try the breathing activity. Perhaps at the start and close of your day will be easiest. Note how you feel prior to beginning. Then, perform the assignment(s). Be sure to note how you feel *after* the deep breathing sessions as well. If you are feeling bold, try a few yoga breaths in public.

Merry Meet the Elements Quick Pick Lesson:
Create Your Own Incense

Making your own incense is both fun and empowering. Often, the ingredients are inexpensive and easy to come by. Depending upon your choices, the tools you will need are few. For dried herbs and resins, a list of required items follows.

A Mortar and Pestle. A mortar is a small bowl, and the pestle is the tool used for grinding substances such as herbs, resins, and spices. Most culinary and magickal stores carry them. I recommend marble or stone as a first choice, because they don't absorb fragrances and often won't stain. Porcelain mortars and pestles are also a fine choice. Although wood is beautiful, you may find that it absorbs fragrance and colors. Modern kitchen witches forgo the old ways and dedicate a **small coffee bean grinder** for grinding herbs and resins. Just remember once you use it for these purposes, you should not use it for anything else.

A ceramic burning bowl. These bowls are used to ensure that your incense burns in a safe place. They can be used for charcoal, stick, or cone incense. Many magickal supplies stores sell these clay bowls and often the heat diffusing sand is included. You may also use dry earth from your garden to fill the bowl and diffuse the heat.

Charcoal Tablets. These are easy lighting and long burning charcoal tablets made especially for burning incense and resins. They are sold by the box and/or roll and are packaged in foil tubes. They are sold at most magickal and smoke shops. DO NOT USE CHARCOAL BRIQUETS.

Suggested Herbs and Resins. Please note this is not a complete list. The herbs and resins I recommend are excellent for the novice and have practical applications for the more experienced practitioner. As you grow in your practice, so too will the contents of your herb cabinet. However, these suggested starters blend well with a variety of scents and are fairly easy to come by.

Key: (H) = Herb (R) = Resin

Dried Lavender Buds (H): **Protection and purification**. The dried buds can be burned directly on the charcoal tablets and emit a sweet, warm fragrance. Lavender mixes well with **Amber** resin **for happiness and love**.

Dried Rose buds (H): **Love and Healing.**

Frankincense (R): Protection, Spirituality, and Strength. Frankincense increases the spiritual vibration of those substances with which it is blended.

Mugwort (H): Spirituality and Psychic Awareness. When burned on charcoal, mugwort emits a smoky, earthy fragrance. Consider adding a pinch of **Frankincense** resin.

Myrrh (R): Balance, Consecration, Purification. When burned, myrrh emits a heavy fragrance. Like Frankincense, it amplifies the spiritual vibration of whatever is blended with it. **Myrrh and Frankincense combined are often used for cleansing, consecration, and representation of Goddess and God energy, respectively.**

White Copal (R): Blessing, Meditation. White Copal has a light almost cedar-like scent. It blends well with all of the suggested herbs and resins. Using your mortar and pestle, you can blend your intent into any number or combination of the above-listed herbs and resins. Simply focus on and state your intent as you blend the contents. When working with resins, blend them down to a powder, as this extends the life of your incense. Once you have completed the mixing phase, be sure to charge the herbs by sifting the contents through your fingers while focusing on your intent. Be creative and use your common scents. ☺

Fire: The Magick of Transformation

For our lesson with fire, we will refer to the guided visualization that follows. You may choose to read over the printed version first, or simply put in the supplemental CD and follow the prompts. Find a time and a place when and where you won't be disturbed. Seat yourself comfortably.

Oya's Fire

See yourself drifting in an ancient sea. Your garments are heavy and cumbersome. They threaten to pull you down into the deep, and only your strength of mind keeps you afloat. You grow weary, allowing the flow of the tide to take you where it will, saving only enough strength to keep your head above water. You lose yourself in the drift, letting the gentle current rock you, the water a womb around you. Then, there is a jarring feeling; the soft rhythm of the water leaves you as your body brushes against the firmness of earth. Stunned, you take in your surroundings. You realize you have washed upon the beach of a lush, tropical isle. Though you have never been here, the land feels familiar. Cool, blue waves break against a white sand beach. They wash over you, revive you.

Your strength returns, and although your garments are water sodden, you walk up the slope that leads from the sea. Sand hot against your feet, you step quickly and with purpose. Above you the raw light of the sun shines down. The sand sparkles and dances at its touch. The air moves in waves in a rhythm matched by the pulse of the sun.

Ahead lies a jungle of trees and vines. You enter this emerald shelter, making your way through the dense growth. Fingers of sunlight poke through the cooling canopy the tall trees provide. Mist rises from the damp earth and mingles with the warm air. Green leaves whisper against your cheek as you pass, leaving drops of dew, like kisses against your skin. Silence surrounds you, and you wonder at the stillness as a feeling of peace envelops you.

Soon, you enter a clearing. You stop, surprised to see an old woman seated before a fire. She wears a robe of black velvet, with ruby red inlays gleaming from the folds like spilled wine in candlelight. She tosses seeds of grain into the fire. Grey wisps of smoke curl into the air as sharp-tongued flames lick the firewood. You duck behind a bush, somewhat fearful of disturbing her. Yet, she raises a hand and beckons you near.

You step close. Under her watchful eye, you are embarrassed by your ruined and cumbersome garments and amazed that she is unaffected by the heat in her heavy velvet robe. She motions for you to sit near, and you do. She holds out her hand to you. In her palm is a seed. As you gaze at the seed, a vision of barren farmland appears. You blink, guessing that your eyes have worked mischief upon you, but the vision remains against the shell of the seed. You realize this is a magickal place and a woman of great magick and power has called you into her realm.

The old woman bids you watch as she flings the seed into the fire. You follow the arc of its movement, and as it lands in the fire, within the smoke there is a vision of a thriving and bountiful land.

She shows you another seed, and as you look, you see your name etched upon it. When she tosses it into the fire, a vision of a woman stirring a cauldron appears. Within that cauldron, you see yourself floating as you had on the sea. You watch, as the story of how you came to be in this magickal place unfolds before your eyes. Loving hands reach down and pluck you from the sea that swells within the cauldron. Gentle and aged hands place you down upon the beach. Grandmother hands wash water over you, revive you. With a loving push, these hands set you on your way toward the jungle, and you see yourself walking to the place you are now.

As quickly as the vision appears, the smoke swallows it. The woman holds out her hands so that you know the hands in the vision are hers. You touch them, and they are as familiar to you as your own, as familiar as the feel of the beach when you first walked upon it.

"Grandmother," you whisper. She nods.

The woman motions for you to stand. She points to your garments and unselfconsciously you strip them away. As you remove each piece of clothing, you see that words are sewn onto the garments. *Fear* marks the first garment, *anger* the second, *insecurity* the third. You lay the garments in a heap at your feet. Wearing only a grey shift, soiled and devoid of color, you stand before this woman of time, so familiar to you.

When she tells you to gather the clothing, you do. Happily, you toss each garment into the fire. As you do, a new outfit rises from the smoke and drifts to your feet as gently as falling ashes. **Fear becomes will. Anger is transformed to peace. Insecurity becomes confidence.** Each garment cleansed, pure, and transformed awaits you.

You bend to gather your new clothes, but the woman stops you, and then points to your shift. She tells you that you cannot don your new clothes. They would not wear well, their beauty and qualities meaningless and lost against the soiled old garment that carries the scent and energy of fear, anger, and insecurity.

"How am I to shed this old, stained shift? I tried to take it off, but it is as if it is sewn to me."

"And so it is, she says. *The shift is all that your life's travels have made of your spirit. To be free of its weight, you too must be transformed."*

She points to the fire. You look, fearful at first, for you know the power of the flame.

"You need not fear that you will be burned," she says. *"Remember when you floated in the ancient sea? The weight of all your worries should surely have dragged you down, yet your will kept you afloat. It is your will and desire to change that shall keep you from burning. Do you believe in your power?"*

You nod, remembering how tired you were, forever drifting in those ancient waters, yet never did you drown, *"I believe,"* you say.

"Speak the magick words and no harm will come to you. Oya, Grandmother of Transformation and Ages, watches over you."

You step to the edge of the fire. Feel the heat against your face. It matches the fire of your spirit. Grey smoke brushes against your cheek, yet it is every bit as cooling as the kiss of dew-covered leaves. You remember the seeds of transformation, your clothing, and you know Oya's fire is a magickal one. Still, with all that you know, and all that you have seen, hesitation weighs heavy upon you. Turning to the old woman, you say, *"You have not taught me the magick words, Grandmother."*

"You have always known them," she says. As you stand at the edge of the fire, the words come and you speak them. It is as if they come from the deepest part of you, the place of knowing. *"Change is mine, if I will it so."* You step forward and pass through the flames to the other side. You emerge from the smoke, wearing a red shift, bright like the first rays of morning sun, pure and unstained by your travels, by your past.

"Life," Grandmother Oya says, and she hands you the garments also transformed by the fire. Over your red shift, which is the mantle of life, you place **Will**, **Peace**, and **Confidence**.

You hug the woman known as Grandmother Oya, give thanks, and offer a twig to feed the fire that transforms, and that cleanses and purifies—the fire that is life—its flames those of will, which keep the life-light burning. As you leave the clearing, you hear the words you always knew. Grandmother's voice rings sweetly in your ears. *"Change is yours if you will it so."*

***

Transformation and change are available to us and ever possible, although walking through fire, even a magickal one, would be both extreme and dangerous. In the visualization, fire and its power serve as metaphors for change. Trial by fire is often the means of our greatest growth spiritually and mentally. How can you grasp the cleansing and transforming powers of fire in the real world? Use the element of fire as part of your magick.

Merry Meet the Elements Quick Pick Lesson:
Candle Transformation Meditation

Color correspondence is an important part of magickal work. By layering your correspondences, you can choose the appropriate color for your magickal work. Whether you are selecting stones, doing chakra work, or candle magick this chart will prove invaluable. Use it as an aid for helping you select the appropriate colored candle for the next lesson.

In the space provided write the following:

> *One aspect of myself/life that I would like to infuse with creativity/transform is...*

Color Correspondence Chart

Color	Purpose
Black	Banishing, uncrossing, ridding space of negativity, and transformation. Goddess energy in the crone aspect.
Blue	Healing, spirituality, creative spirit, communication, intuition, and peace. 5th (Throat) Chakra work.
Brown	Protection and earth rituals. Powers of concentration. Magick for animals.
Gold	Rituals involving god energy, wisdom, and enlightenment. Finding objects. Spirituality.
Green	Earth magick, fertility, money, materialism, healing, success, and luck. Note: the intensity of what you seek to manifest can be affected by the shades of green you choose. For example, dark green can reflect ambition, greed, or jealousy. You can use the shade to intensify or counteract these emotions. 4th (Heart) Chakra work.
Orange	Sensuality, strength, and attraction. 2nd (Sacral) Chakra work.

Color Correspondence Chart (cont.)

Pink	Love, friendship, romance, affection, and femininity.
Purple	Divinatory and highly spiritual work. Power, success, and independence. 6th (Third eye) Chakra work.
Red	Courage, lust, strength, will power, creative spirit, passion, and fertility. Solar festivals. Goddess energy in the mother aspect. 1st (Root) Chakra Work.
Silver	Goddess energy, removal of negativity, and strengthening psychic abilities.
White	Blessings, spirituality, purification, consecrations, protection, and cleansing. Goddess energy in the maiden aspect. May be substituted for most any color, because it is considered universal. 7th (Crown) Chakra work.
Yellow	Charm, enlightenment, friendship, clarity, concentration, confidence, will, and beginnings. 3rd (Solar plexus) Chakra work.

Select a candle color that most closely resonates with what you desire to create or transform. Light the candle daily. Sit before it. Meditate on the aspect you want to actualize. Use your visualization skills and see yourself creating/transforming that which you desire.

Water: The Magick of Flow

Water is one of our most precious resources. As such, water magick is infinitely beneficial. We liken the tides and flow of water to our emotions. Not surprisingly, water represents both the flow of our feelings and our consciousness. The activity that follows places you in touch with the element of water and its cleansing, calming effects.

Peppermint Sea salt Bath for Invigoration

Take this ritual bath whenever you need to feel refreshed and invigorated. Because the water should be tepid to cool, it is not recommended that you take this bath before bedtime. Warm water can be substituted; however, extremely warm temperatures will prove counterproductive.

Please note that although this activity is recommended as a bath, minor adjustments can be made so that a similar effect can be created through showering. Remember that flexibility in your magickal work is always a plus. See the instructions to make the proper adjustments.

Rather than adding a ¼ cup of sea salt to your tub, simply place the container where you can safely and easily reach it from the shower.

Dampen your face cloth or loofah, and dab in the salt as needed. You may add several drops of your essential oil blend to your cloth and follow the bathing instructions outlined, or apply to your damp skin after showering and prior to toweling off.

You will need:

◆ An area to bathe or shower

◆ Face cloth, body buffer, or loofah

◆ A thick, soft towel

◆ ¼ cup of sea salt (Fine grain salt is less abrasive than coarse)

◆ Peppermint essential oil blend

◆ Note the following:

    A. <u>Peppermint is a strong essential oil and known to be an irritant.</u> Try using fewer than the recommended number of drops to start, and then scent according to your preference. **To make any of the oil blends, add 9-15 drops of the essential oil to at least 1 dram/ or roughly ½ ounce of carrier oil**. I recommend **Jojoba oil**, because it is actually a cold pressed wax and will not spoil. Most health food stores carry Jojoba oil as well as the suggested vegetable oils.

B. You can use sweet almond, grape seed, or safflower oils. However, these oils have a limited shelf life.

C. Feel free to substitute any essential oil that you find invigorating. Citrus scents such as grapefruit and orange, or woodsy scents such as bay or cedar may work well, but remember to blend with a carrier oil as outlined above, because mint, citrus, and wood scents can irritate sensitive skin and should therefore be diluted.

Directions:

Add 3 to 9 drops of your chosen essential oil blend and ¼ cup of sea salt to a full tub, or adjust according to shower instructions. Take a moment to blend the salt and oil in the water, and then immerse yourself in the bath. Allow the water to lap over you. Imagine yourself in a cool, blue sea. Breathe deeply. Think about any concerns that may weigh upon you. Each time you exhale, allow the water to wash away these concerns. Draw energy from the cleansing lap of the water.

Next, take your loofah or cloth, and beginning with your feet, rub your skin gently. No harsh strokes. Working your way upward, use the loofah/cloth to massage your body in a circular motion. Lovingly massage your limbs and torso. When you reach your face, take a moment to run some cool water, and then gently splash your face.

After the bath, but while your skin is still damp, apply several drops of your chosen essential oil blend. A complementary lotion may be substituted or used in addition to the oil. Dry yourself and dress. You will feel wonderfully refreshed.

Merry Meet the Elements Quick Pick Lesson: Water
Making Aura Mist

This is a truly fun activity that allows your creativity and common *scents* to run wild! All you need is a 6 to 8 oz. glass spray bottle with a mister, your favorite essential oil, and distilled water. My recommendations for the bottle are amber or cobalt blue; this protects the essential oil from sunlight and disguises the fact that a simple oil and water mixture does not blend. You can purchase the bottles online through bottle supply stores or at fragrance, magickal, specialty, and/or beauty supply shops. Some vendors will sell the bottles with the pump mister as a set, and others will sell them separately. However, the cost of the pump mister is minimal. DO NOT use aluminum or plastic pump bottles because these materials may have a negative reaction with the essential oil.

Directions:

♦ Common sense: Prior to use, always test the essential oil for any skin and/or allergic reactions.

♦ Pour the water into your fragrance bottle. Don't top it off.

♦ Add 15-25 drops of your favorite essential oil, cap it with the pump mister, and then vigorously shake the bottle.

♦ Enjoy using the mist as a personal fragrance or pick-me-up.

♦ You can use it to freshen rooms and linens. Exercise caution when spraying fabrics. Oils can stain.

♦ To minimize this occurrence, always shake the bottle well before using it and spray fabrics from a sensible distance.

Earth: The Magickal Center

Earth magick serves as the springboard for all of our magickal practices. Because we are creatures of the earth, it is our natural center. Earth grounds, energizes, nurtures, and provides the sacred space for all of our magickal endeavors.

I have chosen the following activity because it serves as an excellent introduction to working with earth energy. Additionally, it can become a part of your Ostara Sabbat ritual, where you plant a seed for your intentions and desires, and then work toward harvesting the fruits

of your labor at Mabon.

The Magickal Seed

A. Prepare sacred space. Review Chapter 4 for instructions.

B. Insure that you have all of the stated ingredients handy.

You will need:

♦ A Package of seeds, e.g., flowers or herbs that you enjoy and that

can be grown in pots. Planting directions specific to the seeds you

have chosen can be found on the package. Seeds for small

window gardens work best.

♦ A ceramic pot with potting soil. Prepare this prior to ritual.

♦ (4) Green candles. Mini candles (chime candles) sold at most

magickal stores are the easiest.

Directions:

♦ Once you have prepared your sacred space, select a few seeds

from your package. If specific planting directions are enclosed,

take the required number of seeds.

- Hold the seeds in your palm. Take a moment to visualize what "seed(s)" you wish to plant in your life. Visualize your desire growing to fruition.

- Breathe your intent into the seed(s).

- Hold the planter, and then repeat the process.

- When you have completed your visualization and breathed your intent onto both the seed and the soil, set the planter aside and place the seed on your altar.

- Next, take the (4) green candles. On one carve (ᚠ) Ansuz, the Futhark runic symbol for wisdom. On the second carve (ᛒ) Berkano, the runic symbol for growth. On the third candle carve (ᛉ) Eihwaz, the runic symbol for strength. On the last candle, carve your own magickal symbol, something that holds meaning for you. It should be related to what you wish to plant and reap in your life.

- Place the candles in a circle around the seed and planter.

- Light the candle that symbolizes wisdom and say:

  "Wisdom guide me and all that I plant."

- Light the candle that symbolizes growth and say:

  "In light may my vision grow."

◆ Light the candle that symbolizes strength and say:

> **"With strength and conviction may my vision come into being."**

◆ Light your personal candle and say:

> **"With wisdom, trust, and love I sow a seed to grow strong and in the light of all that is good. My bond with earth be forged, as I nurture and bring this plant into being, and with it my vision. With intent to harm none, the spell is spun, the magick done."**

◆ Plant the seed(s). If possible, maintain the altar setup until the candles burn out. If not, offer thanks, and then snuff the candles. As the plant grows, work toward making your vision a reality. If the seed does not take root, don't lose heart. Rethink your idea and what you envisioned. Perhaps it was not meant to be at that particular time.

Merry Meet the Elements Quick Pick Lesson: Earth Healing and Divination Stones

The ten stones included in the supplemental Spirit Stone kit are your healing/divination stones. They come with their own pouch. The chart enclosed with the stones identifies them by color and properties. You may use them for this activity, and they can also be used for healing Chakra work. If you choose to purchase stones independently, use the color chart provided on pages 87 and 88 to aid in your selection. For the divination activity outlined, make your stone selection from the *Color Chart for Divination Stones* provided on page 98. Use the stones when you desire enlightenment on present or future conditions.

Directions:

♦ Place (9) stones into a cloth pouch. Take a moment to focus on the issue. Narrow down your considerations. For example, what might the day hold? Or what will be the outcome of a particular situation?

♦ Hold the sack of stones in your hand and say:

"Stones of earth, symbolic of wisdom and time,

pave for me a path. Let clarity be mine."

Without peeking, select (1) stone. Use the chart to aid in deciphering the meaning.

Color Chart for Divination Stones

Color	Meaning
Black	Introspection, protection
Blue	Healing
Brown	Material values
Green	Prosperity, money
Orange	Tension
Pink	Love
Red	Passion, arguments
White	Peace, tranquil energy
Yellow	Wisdom, life lessons

As you explore the path, know that you are an active participant. These activities provide an opportunity for practical applications in working with the energy of the elements. To recap: Air is the breath of life. Its lessons aid us in the areas of intellect and communication. The element of fire helps us transform our lives. It brings courage and passion to an endeavor or project. A little candle magick works well when we need a boost in this area. Water teaches us flow. As you may have noticed, magickal baths and creating elixirs are wonderful ways to incorporate water magick. The earth grounds and centers us and teaches patience. Earth magick can be as simple as hugging a tree, using

a stone to ground, or even the act of gardening. Explore the potential

for working with the four elements and use them to help you develop

the potential of the fifth element: Spirit. Remember that Air, Fire,

Water, and Earth serve as both your protectors and your guides. They

aid us in crafting our magick, but they are also forces that can serve to

empower us. We need not wait for moments of magick or spell-work to

call upon the elements. They are readily available to us and eager to

help us find a greater sense of self-reliance and empowerment. For

example, if you have to give a presentation for work or school, why not

call upon the element of air to teach and aid you in the ways of effective

communication? It can be as simple as charging a blue lace agate and

carrying it with you for the event. Use the stone to remind you of the

goals you've set and your intent. It can also serve as a soothing

talisman. No matter where you are in your studies, it is important that

you familiarize yourself with the cornerstones of The Craft, and the

elements are definitely that. Play, explore, and be open to the

possibilities of elemental magick!

Wind, the whisper of life—her breath. Fire, the flame ever burning—her heart. Rain, the gentle flow that washes—her tears. Earth, keeper of ancient secrets and treasures—her body. And we, Her children, live amongst and are—Her spirit.

Notes of a Priestess

Chapter 6

Scent, Psyche, and the Sacred

One way of awakening the magick in your mind is through scent association. Those in The Craft have long known that scent, psyche, and soul share a deep connection. However, science now lends credence to what witches know. An article in Science Daily states, "...researchers from Johns Hopkins University and the Hebrew University in Jerusalem, describe how burning frankincense (resin from the Boswellia plant) activates poorly understood ion channels in the brain to alleviate anxiety or depression." Interestingly, frankincense is ruled by the sun and associated with the warmth, strength, and love of God energy.

The use of herbs is a part of our heritage. The ancients drew from nature, living in harmony with the Great Mother. Their voices whisper to all curious about The Path, to all who seek to flow with the natural tides. As a result, cultures throughout time have used fragrance to evoke emotional responses. Examples include the use of sage in Native American ceremonies as a part of cleansing and blessing rituals, and Southern folk magic calls upon the use of cloves to stem grief. East Indian lore speaks of the use of cinnamon for courage, and we find many more uses for cinnamon throughout the ages. It is beneficial for you to learn to use and manipulate fragrance to forge a deeper connection to your emotions and your magick. In this manner you work more closely with the tables of correspondence, thereby working with the natural flow of energy.

Every plant, planet, and element is a part of the Table of Correspondence. Let's start with the days of week, then move to the planets, zodiac signs, and ultimately the plants that make our magick. Use the herbal chart included in this chapter as a guide. There are many more herbs and plants for each category, and some are interchangeable. For example, both the sun and the moon rule sandalwood. In the chart you will find some of the most common herbs/plants and those that are more easily obtainable. Additionally, our course of study will focus on (7) specific herbs. All are sacred to the witch. You will find many more listed in the Herbal Table of Correspondence. However, the ones chosen can serve you in your everyday needs, and in the application of ritual and magick. Of course, there are hundreds more to learn of and discover. Your journey on The Path will uncover many of the wonders and mysteries the earth holds. Think of yourself as standing at the gate of a garden path. Seven herbs now exist in your garden. If you wish to learn more, plant the seeds through study, work, and a love of nature's treasures.

Herbal Table of Correspondence

Day	Planet	Zodiac	Plants	Intent
Sunday	Sun	Leo	Benzoin, cedar, cinnamon, copal, frankincense, orange, rosemary, sandalwood	God work, healing, protection, illumination, success, magickal power
Monday	Moon	Cancer	Eucalyptus, jasmine, lemon, myrrh, sandalwood,	Goddess work, healing, psychic energy, dreams, soul mate, love
Tuesday	Mars	Aries Scorpio	Allspice, basil, dragon's blood, galangal, ginger, peppermint, wormwood	Legal matters, courage, strength, masculine sexual energy, defensive magick
Wednesday	Mercury	Gemini	Anise, lavender, lemongrass	Communication, business, wisdom, study, divination, harmony
Thursday	Jupiter	Sagittarius Pisces	Cinquefoil, clove, nutmeg, sage	Increase prosperity and spirituality, settle legal matters
Friday	Venus	Taurus Virgo Libra	Cardamom, geranium, orris root, vervain, rose, ylang-ylang	Love, sensuality, beauty, fidelity, happiness, friendship
Saturday	Saturn	Capricorn Aquarius	Comfrey, cypress, patchouli, skullcap	Karmic issues, growth, endings, protection, purification

Rosemary is perhaps one of the oldest of the herbs of The Wise. From the times of Ancient Greece, through the Middle Ages and to the present day, rosemary has been cited for use for anything from remembrance to protection. A popular and hardy herb, rosemary is fragrant and works well in culinary and magickal spells. The herb can be charged with protective intent and sprinkled as spice to a meal. Planting rosemary near the entrance and exit points of a home is thought to ward off mal-intent. The dried herb burns fragrantly and can be used in incense crafted for protection spells. The herb can be carried in a sachet and used to ward off nightmares and protect the unconscious mind in slumber. Refer to your *Herbal Table of Correspondence*, and you will see that the sun rules rosemary. Its day is Sunday. Review the chart and consider other uses for rosemary. By working in correspondence with the day and planetary ruler, you strengthen the power of your work.

The next of our seven herbs is **sandalwood**, whose day is Monday and planetary ruler is the moon. With the moon as its ruler, Monday corresponds to goddess energy, which includes healing work and deepening spiritual connections. Like rosemary, sandalwood has an ancient and renowned history. When working with sandalwood, think along the lines of healing, purification, and blessings. Sandalwood possesses a deeply cleansing and pleasing scent. Though I have included it under herbs, you can find fragrant sandalwood in the form of woodchips. These can be burned in the fire or on specially designed charcoals. In this way sandalwood can be used to prepare a sacred space for healing work. Sandalwood chips can also be added to sachets and mojo bags. These sachets/bags can be empowered with a healing spell. When carried, sandalwood promotes a deeper spiritual connection.

Mars rules Tuesday. Energy aspects of this day include resolving legal matters and business affairs, taking initiative and behaving assertively, tapping into the male or Yang energy and working toward our desires. **Galangal** is an excellent herb to complement these correspondences. One can carry Galangal root in a mojo bag when dealing with court or legal issues. The ground root can also be added to incense ingredients to promote protection.

One of the most beloved herbs in magickal lore is **lavender**. Like its planetary ruler, Mercury, which rules Wednesday, lavender is versatile. It possesses many magickal, medicinal, and aroma-therapeutic associations. Of the different varieties of lavender, English and French

Lavender are wonderfully fragrant. From a magickal standpoint, lavender can be used for healing, cleansing, and purifying. Additionally, the herb can be employed as a calmative and as a stimulant. Lavender is capable of possessing seemingly contradictory properties because it is an adaptogenic herb, which means that it will work to create balance by instigating the proper bodily reaction. Because Mercury is considered a temperamental planet, hence "mercurial" tendencies, it is important to make use of an element that promotes balance. Consider burning dried lavender to create a harmonious environment and/or to promote purification and protection of an area. It also works well added to sachets. A sachet placed under the pillow can promote restful sleep. At the close of this chapter, you will find the *Lavender Fields Meditation*. You may use the supplemental guided meditation CD. Enjoy!

Jupiter is the planetary ruler for **cinquefoil,** also known as Five Finger Grass. Its corresponding day is Thursday. Think of the energetic properties of the planet Jupiter in terms of increase or expansion. Likewise, cinquefoil is regarded in terms of five fingers reaching out toward desires or goals. The herb is most commonly used in spells or rituals involving money or highly prized possessions. Consider the recipe that follows for granting a desire for money or abundance.

Recipe with Spell

Add **3 parts cinquefoil** to **2 parts myrrh resin** and **1 part patchouli leaf**. Grind the herbs and resin in a mortal and pestle. As you do so, envision your desire. Breathe your intent into the mixture, then place it in a small, approximately 2"x2", green cloth sachet or pouch. Place the pouch on your altar. Light a green candle, and then meditate on your intent for several minutes. Draw prosperity symbols upon the pouch. Dollar signs, the glyph for the planet Jupiter or the Futhark Rune for prosperity can serve as some ideas. Thank Universe and then snuff the candle. Carry the pouch with you as a reminder of your goals toward prosperity.

The spell is best accomplished when the moon is waxing to full. You can perform it on a Thursday, during the waxing phase, but be clear on your intent. Jupiter represents increase, although it will inflate issues that you have failed to reconcile. In other words, if you have yet to set your financial house in order, do so. In that way you will not work against the energetic flow.

Because it is ruled by the element of water and the planet Venus, **orrisroot** is commonly associated with love. Friday falls under the rule of

Venus and is therefore an excellent day to do spell-work involving matters of the heart. Both the Goddess Venus and the corresponding planet, Venus, are associated with beauty, love, and the power of attraction. The planet is symbolic of romance, the arts, and pleasure. These energies should not be trifled with, nor should they be taken lightly.

This is a good place to segue into a discussion about two of the greatest gifts given to us as humans: (1) the ability to reason, and (2) freewill. How does this tie into Friday, love, orrisroot, and Venus? Well, let's think for a moment. The ability to reason means that we possess the skills needed to make logical, informed decisions and choices. Freewill means that we possess the ability to make choices for ourselves. Freewill **IS NOT** imposing our will upon others. That's how this ties into what it means to perform any spell-work, not just those spells involving love. In short: Do not impinge upon another's freewill. What this means for you and love spells is DO NOT WORK A SPELL TO CAUSE ANOTHER TO FALL IN LOVE WITH YOU. Whether or not you get what you think you want, you will definitely get more than you bargained for. Why? You will have acted against someone else's freewill and coerced love, which in the end isn't love at all. Why am I so heated about this? Over the course of twenty years of practice, countless

people have asked me for love spells. Few have wanted to abide by the

rules of freewill. When I have refused to work the spells they desired,

they have done so on their own with disastrous results. I have grown

tired of people attempting to use magick and its properties to justify

their own selfish needs and ends. Think about it. How would you feel if

you were coerced into love? You have freewill, and that gives you the

right to *choose whom you will and will not* share your affections with.

Imagine being stripped of that right. There may be other books and

traditions that contradict all that I've said. And as a creature of freewill,

you are more than welcome to pursue those paths. However, do not go

blindly. Remember, you have read this far because you have chosen to.

No one is *forcing* you. Now consider a world without freewill, a world

where you are forced to read this book. What information and

opportunities might you miss? Even as the author of these "outlaw"

teachings, I would not consciously choose to live in that world. So, why

would someone tell you that it is perfectly okay to strip another human

being of his/her right to choose? Because it sells! Many people desire

the path of least resistance, the easy fix. Don't exercise to be fit and

slim, take a pill. Don't work on fixing your issues, just get someone to love you and it will all be okay. That's a tentative existence, because at the end of the day, no matter what your faith or what path you choose, you will be held accountable for your choices and your actions. Karma works by the laws of nature and is completely unbiased.

Okay, I am over my rant; now, back to orrisroot. Spells and magick involving orrisroot require the empowerment of the root for the purpose of love. Often the person will either carry the root to attract love, or give it to the person whose affections they wish to receive. This gift may only be given with the person's full awareness and permission. Orrisroot can be powdered, made into sachets, or sprinkled onto sheets. It possesses an aroma not unlike violets. In keeping with the versatility of Venus, the root can also be made into a pendulum for divinatory purposes or used as a token of protection.

Saturday is named for the Roman god, Saturn, and is associated with time and karma. As you may have guessed, the planet Saturn is also this day's planetary ruler. When choosing an herb to work with consider **cypress**, which is governed by Saturn. It works well in matters involving karmic issues, growth, endings, prosperity, protection, and/or purification. Cypress possesses a pleasing, woodsy fragrance. The bark can be obtained in its natural state and is usually sold under the category of resins. Burned on charcoal, it is used to enhance prayer and ritual work, adding energy to the desired magickal working. The scent of cypress is deeply calming. When mixed with copal, another resin governed by Saturn, the blend can be used to enhance meditative states and help one to sort through karmic and past life issues. The woody and earthy scents play upon our sense of smell, harkening to a distant, yet somehow familiar, time when we were in harmony with nature and the earth.

If you shy from incense, consider using cypress in a protection mojo bag. This will require a bit of planning.* For best results work the spell on the night of the full moon. If you require protection sooner, you may follow the instructions, omitting the aspect of charging the coin beneath the full moon.

*A note on the moon and spell-work

The energy of the moon in each of its three phases directly correlates with the name of the phase: waxing, full, and waning. Be sure to tailor your spell-work accordingly. Work toward increase during waxing and full. This is why you are charging your coin on the full moon. If spell-work must be performed during the waning phase, work toward removing (decreasing) obstacles.

Mojo Bag

Make or purchase a **black flannel bag**. It need not be any bigger than 3" x 3." It can be smaller if desired. Using a **silver marker**, these can be purchased at most any art or office supply store, draw onto the bag any/or all of the symbols shown for protection. From left to right: The Futhark rune symbol for protection, the Pentagram, the Hamsa.

Alternatively, you may research and draw any symbol of protection that speaks to you.

You will need:

♦ A black candle

♦ A bit of cypress resin

♦ An obsidian stone

♦ (1) Silver coin. A Kennedy Half Dollar, or an old quarter from the silver standard era will work wonderfully. However, it is the representation of silver that is important. Any "silver" coin will do.

Directions

♦ Cleanse the stone and the coin in spring water and sea salt to wash away the energy of others. Dry each thoroughly. Breathe your intent for protection onto the coin before charging it.

♦ Charge the silver coin by allowing it to sit in the light of the full moon. You need not charge it more than a few minutes.

♦ Breathe your intent of protection into the stone as well, though you will NOT charge it in the moonlight. You are charging the *coin* only to enhance the magickal associations between silver and moonlight.

♦ Place the coin, cypress resin, and obsidian into the bag. Light the black candle, and then place it within your sacred space. Sit before the candle for a moment and visualize yourself within a protective circle. See the black candle standing tall behind you. It illuminates a protective ring of flame and shines its light into the darkness beyond. See yourself within this protective circle. Envision and welcome within this space your guardians, totem animals, or any energy you find protective. Be comforted by the light that shines above and around you. Meditate on the idea of the light both illuminating and burning away those forces that may harm you, while the black of the candle absorbs all negative energy. Hold the protective bag during this meditation and feed the energy of the visualization into the bag. When you are ready, snuff the candle, thank the guardians, and keep the bag with you. *It is important to note that no magick can serve as the replacement for common sense. Use the Mojo Bag to heighten your sense of awareness. Do not take unnecessary chances or become careless.*

***

Working with herbs is a part of our heritage and history. It is a dying art, as many look to quick fix remedies for help. Yet, we are of the earth. Its bounty is the stock and trade of our wellbeing and our magick. Aspirin is a derivative of the Willow. Kava is a natural sedative. There was a time when the woods and forests were our pharmacies. The shamans, priestesses, priests, and medicine men of old knew what plants would heal and what would harm. Failure to familiarize ourselves with nature is to deprive ourselves of vital aspects of our birthright. It is not within the scope of this book to cover the history and wonders of

herbal healing and plant medicine. However, as Wiccans we should

study the work of the shamans and those versed in earth magick.

Astrotheology and Shamanism, by Jan Irvin & Andrew Rutajlt, *Plants of*

the Gods, by Schultes Hofmann & Rätsch & *Witchcraft Medicine* by

Müller-Ebeling, Rätsch and Storl are well-written and researched texts

worth delving into.

I have referenced lavender and its adaptogenic properties. Now,

let's use the following activity to learn a bit about the effects and the

power of scents. You will discover the *Lavender Fields Meditation* in

print on the following pages and on the supplemental CD. Find a time

and a place where you will not be disturbed. Ensure that you have all

necessary items. Enjoy.

Lavender Fields Meditation

You will need:

♦ (1) Sprig of fresh English or French Lavender, or lavender essential oil. Crushed, dried lavender will work as well.

    a. If using dried lavender, you may want to bundle it in cheesecloth, or keep it in a glass jar for this activity. You can uncap the jar to inhale the fragrance, and then recap it to store the herb.

    b. In the absence of plant material, a small vial of lavender essential oil is fine. Because it is highly concentrated, do not apply the essential oil to your skin. Instead, dilute it in a carrier oil such as jojoba or apricot oil. Or, you may place several drops of the pure oil on a cotton ball. Although the meditation is performed with lavender, any fragrance that you find uplifting and positive can be substituted. Ensure that you modify the visualization to follow suit.

♦ (1) Purple Candle

Find a quiet space. Light a candle of the appropriate color. If you are working with lavender, use purple. Allow yourself to be lulled and relaxed by the dance of the candle's flame. Blink naturally and clear your mind. When you feel sufficiently relaxed, take the lavender in your hands and gently inhale the fragrance.

Visualization

See yourself in a lush green field. All around you lavender grows. Above you, white clouds drift lazily against a blue sky.

You stand in the field, your arms outstretched. Allow the lavender scented wind to blow through your hair.

(Pause)

Feel the wind's caress against your skin. Slowly turn clockwise, letting the fragrant wind envelop your being.

(Pause)

Breathe deeply. The heady scent of lavender becomes a part of you, and you feel cleansed, renewed. The fragrance seeps into your consciousness, washing away tension and worry. The scent of lavender replaces these feelings with its strong and cleansing breath. Breathe in the fragrance and feel your mind clear.

(Pause)

Move through the field, feeling a kinship with the plant that grows around you. The sun is warm against your face. As it shines, warming the earth, the scent of lavender is released. Each step you take intensifies the heady fragrance rising from the earth.

As you reach the edge of the field, pause and breathe deeply.

The space of your mind is cleansed and refreshed. Your body and spirit are renewed. Hold fast to the scent of the fragrance.

(Pause)

Take time to thank the earth for its beauty and gifts.

Take time to bask in the warm sunlight, the sweet air.

(Pause)

Now follow the path that will lead you home.

After you draw yourself from the meditation, thank the candle flame for guiding you to a place of peace. Snuff the candle. Take a moment to ground any energy you may have raised. **Bright Blessings!**

It is from the ancient ones, the old ways, that we gain our power. Within the circle, we are timeless. All things are possible. All of ritual begins.

Notes of a Priestess

Chapter 7

Winding the Silver Path

Wicca follows the Wheel of the Year and the cycles of the moon. In this chapter we will focus upon a 12-moon cycle. Once you are comfortable with the energy of the rituals provided, feel free to write a ritual for the Blue Moon. Remember, the Blue Moon is the 2nd full moon in a month, and it accounts for the 13-moon cycle.

Take a look at *Circle of the Silver Path's* Lunar Year. This guide provides the twelve months of the year and the corresponding names of the moon as taught in my tradition. Don't worry if the names and correspondence list differ from others you come across. Wicca is a fluid religion. Every tradition will identify with those names that most closely mirror their roots. These are the names by which our circle recognizes each moon.

Circle of the Silver Path's Moon Chart

Month	Moon	Reason
January	Wolf Moon	Protector of hearth and home
February	Ice Moon	Bloom beneath the ice
March	Storm Moon	Winds of change
April	Growing Moon	Planting seeds of change
May	Flower Moon	Buds of promise
June	Mead Moon	Celebration of herbs/nature
July	Blessing Moon	Relaxed energy and a time to reflect on our blessings
August	Corn Moon	1st Harvest, we reap what we sow
September	Harvest Moon	Main harvest and Mabon/Witches' Thanksgiving
October	Blood Moon	Final harvest/sacrifice
November	Snow Moon	Northern Hemisphere/ retreat and reflection
December	Cold Moon	Winter/entering a period of renewal

The rituals provided are unique to Circle of the Silver Path's teachings. I want you to come away with a sense of belonging, not just that you have read another book on Wicca. Many of us know that this can be a very solitary path. Often, without coven membership, it becomes difficult to find a sense of communion with others of similar spiritual beliefs. Because this is a primer, I will provide you with authentic rituals that you can personalize and develop as your own celebration of the moon cycles. Go!

Healing Waters
A Ritual Meditation for Every Moon

The basics of all magickal practice begin with cleansing and creating sacred space. Mind and body are the most powerful magickal instruments we possess. Treat your mind, body, and spirit to a feast of the senses with a magickal meditation and cleansing bath as part of, or prior to, every full moon ritual. Immerse yourself in the wondrous healing powers of the elements and enhance your ability to focus and project energy by attuning the most sacred of your magickal tools.

Here's how:

For bathing rituals, ideally you need a bathtub, but remember, these bathing rituals can be adapted to showers or most any water source. Additionally, you can perform this as a seated ritual by employing a representation of water in a glass dish or crystal bowl.

You will need:

♦ A favorite stone

♦ A supply of colored candles. Each month will dictate, so read before you begin.

♦ Relaxing music. I recommend soothing instrumentals such as: yoga, meditation, or massage music.

♦ Your favorite incense

♦ Sea salt

Important Note: For each of the months I will suggest a specific oil and stone. These are optional additions to your repertoire. They add dimension and richness to your work, but are not essential. Take your time in acquiring your tools, so that your practice does not become financially exhaustive. Additionally, if you do not have access to colored candles, a white candle works as well. If you decide to use the oils and stones, follow these directions.

Use of Oil: Before using any oil, test for skin sensitivity or allergic reaction. This can be accomplished by placing a small drop on the inside of the wrist. Wait 24 hours. If there is no reaction, add (3) drops to your bath water. Remember that some oils are irritants; so, even if you love the smell, don't go overboard. If you prefer not to add the oil to your bath, use it to anoint your candles. To do so, place a drop of oil on the middle of the candle. Rub the oil toward the wick, and then returning to the middle of the candle, rub down toward the base. <u>Always move in one direction when applying the oil, rather than back and forth.</u> As you anoint the candle, focus on the energy of the moon and the intent of the ritual. Lastly, for any oil recommended, corresponding incense can be substituted.

Use of Stone: The stone is a tool of focus and adds energy to your ritual. Whether you choose to perform this as a bathing or seated ritual, hold the stone as you meditate. Envision the color and energy of the stone moving from your hand and pulsing through your body. Allow your fingers to roll over the smooth surface of the stone as you repeat the meditation. If you choose to perform the ritual as a bath, you may leave the stone in the water as you relax and focus on your intent.

Before you begin: Review the elements of "**Casting a Pagan Circle**" in **Chapter 4.** Remember to clear your workspace of any lingering energy by smudging with sage or using one of the sacred space spritzers. Light your favorite incense and ensure that you ground and center. Have your music cued and ready. If you have not memorized the meditation, have it readily available. You can either copy it onto a slip of paper or record it.

If you choose to perform the bathing ritual, be safe and don't place electrical devices near water. Instead, upon completion of the meditation, allow the music to play in the background as you are toweling off.

If you opt not to perform this as a bathing ritual, ensure that you have water represented in a glass dish or crystal bowl, and that you are comfortably seated with your tools available. Again, the music is to ease you into a relaxed frame of mind. You may play it while you are creating sacred space or relax to it after the ritual.

When you are ready to close, allow the energy of the meditation, the music, and the moon to flow through you. Take your time and thank the elements upon conclusion of the ritual.

January: Wolf Moon

January marks the Wolf Moon, a moon of power. The focus changes from introspection to an awareness of the world outside. We model after the wisdom of the wolf and are reminded of the importance of our pack/those closest to us.

CANDLE: White

OIL: Sandalwood

FOCUS: Planning

STONE: Citrine for protection against negativity

Meditation:

Universe, help me to weave a web of protection that keeps those I love safe within my magick and care. As the wolf is with its pack, so I am with my loved ones: loyal, loving, and faithful for life.

February: Ice Moon

The full moon in February coincides with the quickening energy of Imbolc. Similarly, beneath the ice, earth prepares for the blossoming of spring. As we plan in February, we hope to see those plans realized beneath the watch of the moon.

CANDLE: Blue

OIL: Lavender

FOCUS: Making plans, inner and spiritual growth, self-love

STONE: Rose quartz for self-love, healing, and wellbeing

Meditation:

If I am confident about my actions and myself, I am confident in my world. As I rest within the womb of the mother, recharge me with her love, energy, and strength that I may love myself and share this love with others.

March: Storm Moon

The energy of March's moon cleanses away debris and clears a path for change. Working with the energy of Ostara, the Storm Moon lights a path for us.

CANDLE: Green

OIL: Ylang-Ylang

FOCUS: Balance, new beginnings, recognizing self- truths

STONE: Obsidian for facilitating change

Meditation:

As the storms pass, I am renewed. I see within and without. I plant within and without. Goodness grows within me, as within, so without. With each day, I bring balance to my life and being.

April: Growing Moon

The April moon is a hopeful, happy moon. Take advantage of its energies and nurture those around you, your ideas, and yourself.

CANDLE: Gold

OIL: Bergamot or Patchouli

FOCUS: Strength of mind, grounding, and nurture

STONE: Hematite for grounding

Meditation:

I am filled with hope as I work toward crafting my reality. Grant me the power to be all that I am meant to be.

May: Flower Moon

May's Flower Moon is filled with bright energy. Its spirit dovetails with Beltane, the union of The Lady and The Lord. It reminds us that the blessings and bounty of nature surround us.

CANDLE: Green

OIL: Sandalwood

FOCUS: Creative interaction

STONE: Carnelian

Meditation:

Earth and water, fire and air, all elements are gathered. I call upon each to share the magick of this moment with me. Strengthen my spirit and self. Help me to see and share your wonders, your powers. Gracious Goddess, Gracious God, teach me responsible interaction with the elements, that I may build a fertile and creative relationship with them.

June: Mead Moon

Grab a goblet; it's the Mead Moon! The full moon of June marks lunar strength. Whereas, Litha, which is celebrated in June, marks the

Summer Solstice, the longest day of the year.

CANDLE: Orange

OIL: Rose Geranium

FOCUS: Strength, decision making

STONE: Amazonite for courage

Meditation:

I stand in a field, abundant and green, my mind open to all possibilities. I realize that informed decisions require an open mind. Let me use this time within the womb of the Great Mother to gain perspective. Provide me with the strength of mind to make decisions that are right for my path.

July: Blessing Moon

After time spent planning and working, July's full moon reminds us that it is time to reflect upon our blessings. It is a time to check in with our intuition and give thanks for its guiding light.

CANDLE: Silver

OIL: Jasmine

FOCUS: Intuition and path-working

STONE: Moonstone for intuition

Meditation:

Through dreams, meditation, and my daily path let me pave my way to successful ventures. All that I am, I choose to be. I can, because I believe. I believe, because of who I am.

August: Corn Moon

The Corn Moon of August brings with it a special golden-laced intensity, as lunar and solar energy work in harmony with the Sabbat Lughnasadh.

CANDLE: Yellow

OIL: Frankincense

FOCUS: Vitality

STONE: Sunstone for regeneration and vitality

Meditation:

Let me drink of earth's energy, be renewed by the sun's rays. Let me enjoy my successes, reflect upon my shortcomings, and grow strong from the lessons learned. Let me store my energy and prepare for yet another turn of the wheel.

September: Harvest Moon

As we bask beneath the rays of the Harvest Moon, we see the wheel has neared a full turn. We are in the dark time of the year and must once again look within. As we embrace the Harvest Moon, we employ the energies of Mabon and seek balance.

CANDLE: (1) Brown (1) Yellow

OIL: Ylang Ylang

FOCUS: Balance

STONE: Sugilite for integration between the spiritual and physical realms

Meditation:

Gracious Goddess, Gracious God, help me to find my balance and my place between the world of men and the realm of spirit. Let me move freely within and between the worlds, ever knowing my place in both.

October: Blood Moon

The Blood Moon of October works with the energy of Samhain, the witches' New Year. What better time to immerse in the warm, bathing waters of the mother's womb and shed that which we no longer need.

Candle: (1) Black (1) Red

Oil: Dragon's Blood

Focus: Healing and the need for equilibrium

Stone: Bloodstone for balance

MEDITATION:

Here, I release to the Great Mother that which I no longer need. As the waters flow, so my needs flow to the source of all life and all release. Within these waters, within the womb of the mother, I seek inner harmony and balance.

November: Snow Moon

Because our tradition is Celtic-eclectic, we know November's moon as the Snow Moon. Here, in Oregon, that makes sense. However, Wiccan lore also refers to this moon as the Mourning Moon. Just as snowfall blankets the earth and signals the need to draw inside, this moon by either name is a moon of withdrawal and introspection. Like the season, we turn within.

CANDLE: (1) White (1) Black

OIL: Cedar

FOCUS: Change

STONE: Labradorite for transformation and communication

MEDITATION:

Gracious Goddess, gracious God, here within these healing waters, I reach out to you. Help me to see within, that I may know myself, and to shine light upon that which I would transform. Grant me strength for positive choice and change. Allow me a closer link to you.

December: Cold Moon

As the wheel turns we move deeper into the season, and our path takes us beneath the silver rays of December's Cold Moon. This very special full moon falls within the month of the Yule Sabbat. We celebrate the energy of The Lady and The Lord on many levels, for here the reign of the Crone ends as the Mother gives birth and the Maiden attends. We witness the birth of the Lord of Light. Yule marks the vanquishing of the Holly King and the return of the Oak King. It is the promise of winter's end.

CANDLE: (1) White (1) Red (1) Black

OIL: Frankincense**/Myrrh**

FOCUS: Path-working

STONE: Fluorite for integration

** *These are expensive oils. You can substitute with a Frankincense and Myrrh incense. If you use the oils, do not apply them to your bath or skin.*

Meditation:

Great Mother, birth me anew and help me to find my path and purpose on all planes. Let me realize my spiritual and mundane potential. Let me walk each path with pride and integrity. Allow tides to turn as they will. Allow me light within darkness. Allow me the tools to guide and be guided. Birth me anew and with purpose.

We have circled *The Wheel of the Year*. If you chose some of the options such as the stones, then you have gathered all four elements

around you in your rituals. Incense for *Air,* candlelight for *Fire*, *Water*,

either in representation or the bath, and stones for *Earth*. Use the

rituals and build upon them as you deepen your practice of Wicca.

In shaded groves and forests dark, beneath The Lady's silver gaze, the rhythm of the turning wheel keeps time. Its pulse, our drum; we heed the call. Drawn to the Ancient Ones, the ancient ways, our dance keeps time with all eternity.

Notes of a Priestess

Chapter 8

In Shaded Groves:

A Ritual for Every Sabbat

Celebration of the sabbats lies at the heart of our practice. As we know, they reflect the Wheel of the Year and exemplify attunement with natural cycles. In Chapter 2, we learned the names and dates of the sabbats. We have learned how to layer our correspondences and how to create sacred space. Here, you will find a ritual for each of the eight sabbats in Wicca. These rituals allow you to cast a pagan circle, which is the creation of sacred space to perform and contain magickal work. It differs from a Wiccan circle in that the intricacies of casting formal circle are a part of the Wiccan mysteries. As a High Priestess, I cannot divulge these aspects to the uninitiated. However, each rite is designed to provide you with a foundation that you can draw from and build upon. Each will work for the solitary practitioner, or can be adapted for a group. If you are working solitary, adjust the words provided so that they suit you. If you are working with a group, remember to adjust the tools needed for the group and adjust the wording and delegation of responsibilities to suit the needs and size of the group. For those interested in learning more about the mysteries, initiation, or becoming a member of the clergy, refer to the information on self-initiation and classes with Circle of the Silver Path at the end of Chapter 9.

Enter into ritual work in the proper frame of mind, because the goal of ritual is to shift our consciousness so that we are in touch with and nurturing the Higher Self. We want to move focus away from everyday concerns and awaken to the freedom of our spirituality. Cleanse and prepare yourself for ritual by using one of the ritual baths in Chapter 7. Remember, the baths can be modified to encompass showering. Of course there are times when we want to perform ritual, but our schedules don't afford us all of the time we need. You don't need to sacrifice ritual. Instead, become creative. If you only have time to splash cold water on your face, then do so. Perhaps you can use one of the suggestions provided in Chapter 4 to create a cleansing spritzer that you can use to refresh your face and body. Just remember that preparation of the self is the first step in spiritual attunement. We want to create and enter our sacred space, having washed away the weight of mundane concerns.

Your circle and magick gain power through the repetition and evolution of your practice. However, ritual is not an act of rote memorization. In this chapter, you will find worksheets where you can write your own consecrations and quarter calls. The consecration of the circle portends the ideals embodied in the ritual. You further add dimension and richness to your practice by always writing calls that are specific to the energy and purpose of the rite. In the paragraphs that follow, I will provide a brief explanation about key aspects of writing and performing ritual. A detailed explanation of preparation for your spiritual work follows those paragraphs.

About the Consecration:

You don't have to be poetically inclined to write consecrations and quarter calls. You must simply speak from the heart. Think of the reason for celebrating the sabbat. Think of what you hope to accomplish. These ideas are the basis for your consecration. For example, if we were to write a consecration for our Imbolc rite, it might look something like this:

Awaken from winter's dark night. If we are to plant the seeds of change, then we must lure the light.

Do you have to rhyme? Absolutely not! Often, witches create rhymes because they are easier to remember. Write in the style that suits you. It can be long or short, just ensure that you get to the point. Meaning, your consecration dedicates the work of the circle. It states in simple terms why you have gathered for the rite.

About Quarter Calls

Much the same is true of quarter calls. In order to write them you must first think of the element you are addressing. What are the qualities it possesses? What are you asking of the quarters? How does their presence relate to the energy of the ritual? Will you address the elemental rulers as outlined in the Silver Path tradition? How will you thank them at the close of ritual? In this section, we will review sample quarter calls and their corresponding dismissals. Each will provide a slight variation on the theme.

Your quarter calls can and should be longer than your consecration, but again, avoid an essay and keep to the point. In some examples, I will include the name of the corresponding elemental ruler.

It is always your choice as to whether or not you address them specifically. You may choose simply to refer to the "guardians." However you choose to address the elements and the corresponding elementals, the most important point is that you do so with reverence.

Sample Quarter Calls

East: *Guardians of the east. Sylphs of air and springtime gay, we call upon your presence this day. Your energy brings newness to all gathered here. We face the winds of change, spirits light and free of fear.*

Closing: *Spirits of air, thank you for your springtime currents of energy. With reverence we bid thee farewell and blessed be.*

South: *Mighty Djinn, dragons and salamanders, spirits of firelight, bring to us a passion bright. We seek change and awakenings, a chance to start anew. Bring us courage and will to see our desires through.*

Closing: *Mighty Djinn and keepers of the sacred flame, we thank you for the courage, will, and desire to see our dreams through. For your blessings and protection, ever are we grateful. Now, we bid thee farewell and blessed be.*

West: *Undines and mermaids, water creatures all—hear us now; answer our call. You flow within the stream of all consciousness and emotions, grant us the energy to pursue change with devotion.*

Closing: *Guardians of the west, we thank you for allowing us the depth of emotion needed to glimpse the awakening of our inner selves. May we flow with grace and ease upon the currents of change we have wrought. Our thanks as we bid thee farewell and blessed be.*

North: *Wise Gob, keeper of gnomes and bears, protector of woodland spirits fair, your energy is the life pulse of our earth mother, provide us the power to nurture one another.*

Closing: *Guardians of the north, wise Gob and creatures of earth, we thank you for the strength and guidance to nurture one another and our dreams. We honor you, and the land, which is the body of the Mother. Bright blessings as we bid thee hail and farewell.*

***

In writing quarter calls, often inspiration comes from simply spending time with the elements. Relax. Allow them to speak to you.

About Bringing Power to the Circle

Once circle has been cast and the quarters have been called, we move into the elements of ritual. Bringing power to the circle is important because this is the energy that you will draw from for the work that you do within circle. It is the process of raising positive energy to empower the participants as well as the work of the circle. When casting formal circle, witches will often refer to this as "raising the cone of power." For our pagan circle, there are some modifications. I have provided a simple chant designed to awaken energy within the chanter. As you recite the words, let go. Allow yourself to feel the energy rise within you. I've found that it works best if you begin a slow recitation, and as you feel the energy rise, allow this to be reflected in the pace of your chant. Have fun. Sing and dance. Allow your joy and personal empowerment to fill your words.

About the Invitation to The God and Goddess

It's important to note the difference between an invitation and an invocation. In the rituals provided, we offer an *invitation* to The Lord and Lady. We ask their presence, guidance, and protection in our circle. In formal Wiccan circle, the High Priestess and/or High Priest perform an invocation, where they call forth and internalize the energy of The Lord and Lady. If a High Priestess and High Priest are working together in circle, then the High Priestess will call forth (invoke) the High Priest with God energy, and the High Priest will invoke the High Priestess with Goddess energy. This is a much more advanced practice and is not recommended unless you have had training in sending, directing, and internalizing energy.

For our invitation, we invite god energy into our circle first. This is done so that The Lord, as consort, may prepare a path for The Lady. After we extend the invitation to The Lord, we light his candle in recognition of his energy and presence, and then extend an invitation to The Lady, subsequently lighting her candle as well. When we close circle and thank both god and goddess for their presence, we extinguish the god candle first, for the same reasons of preparing a path, and then extinguish the goddess candle. You will find that the invitation for our rituals is a brief rhyme that is easy to remember. As you become more comfortable with the rituals, you can modify the invitation or create your own. Simply remember that your request should be respectful and reflect the overall import of the circle.

About the Message

The message, or mystery as it is referred to in formal circle, is the heart of your ritual. It speaks to the purpose of the circle and directs the intent. Each message in the rituals provided explains the reason for gathering, the meaning of the sabbat, and how the sabbat relates to the lesson that follows. The structure is such that the message can be tailored to those working alone or in a group. If you are working solitary, this is the aspect of ritual that you read and internalize. If you are working with others, then the circle leader recites the message to the participants.

About the Lesson

The lesson is the actual work that you perform during the ritual. It is a form of working magick because you seek to use the elements available to you to create change. The lesson may take the form of a spell, a prayer, or any combination of magickal undertakings. The lesson will always center on the energetic focus of the ritual. For example, the energy of Imbolc focuses on beginnings; therefore the lesson for this sabbat will share a similar theme.

About Sharing

If working solitary, the sharing aspect of ritual is an opportunity to commune with the energies we have called forth and to give thanks for the bounty we are blessed with. When working with a group, sharing encompasses the attributes above, as well as the opportunity to commune with one another. The partaking of the sacrament is the first step in grounding the energy we have raised. It also offers an opportunity for private or shared reflection.

We never eat the last of the sacrament. Instead, we save a small offering to share with the elements. This is a symbolic acknowledgment and thanks to deity for the blessings of life so generously provided.

About Closing the Circle

When closing down circle, we first give thanks to The Lord and The Lady for their attendance. Speak from the heart, and then snuff the god candle so that an energetic path is prepared for The Lady. Next, snuff the goddess candle. Some traditions advocate pinching the wick with the fingers, others use a candlesnuffer, and still others blow out the candle. Any method that you are comfortable with is fine. There are myths that blowing out a candle is bad luck or disrespectful. Let's dispel that myth. Goddess and God exist within each of us. Our breath is the life force and it is sacred. It is neither bad luck nor disrespectful to acknowledge deity and/or the elements with our breath, for we speak their names and praises with this same breath.

A word about Grounding

We ground and close down the chakras so that we are not filled with restless energy. Just as we drew energy from the earth to empower us, we want to envision returning that energy to the earth for use at another time. Presently, I will address the basics of closing the chakras. However, in the pages that follow, you will find a detailed explanation of how to employ the chakras for the purposes of receiving and grounding energy. Where grounding is concerned, we close our chakras from the crown to the root. As we envision the covering of the chakras, it helps if we picture the energy flowing downward, returning to the earth.

Beginning with the Crown Chakra, we see the spinning ball of light slowing, and then stopping. See each chakra protected and safely covered. It helps me to envision the chakra lights being placed in a box and then drawing a curtain closed around the box. Use whatever visualization works for you. Just ensure that when you **close** your

chakras, you begin at the crown, working your way down to the 3rd Eye,

Throat, Heart, Solar plexus, and Sacral Chakras, ending at the Root

Chakra.

About the Closing Chant

As part of our closing, we offer a chant that is designed to release

any energies we have drawn into circle. In this way our sacred space no

longer serves as a work area. Instead, we return it to a place of peace.

The Offering and Opening of Circle

Once you have completed the chant, the circle is open and ritual

is officially over. However, if you recall, we saved an offering for deity

and the elements. Pick up the small serving of cakes and beverage that

you saved. Take them outside, offer them up to the sky, and then

sprinkle the offering upon the earth. You may do so comfortably and

discreetly in your yard, or a place you have designated that feels safe

and right for you. Be respectful of the environment as you pour the

beverage and sprinkle the crumbs. This is symbolic of giving back to

nature the gifts and the bounty shared with us. If you cannot go outside, perhaps you can set the offering on a window ledge.

The circle is now closed and all energy raised has been properly channeled and grounded. Take time and care in putting your tools away. Remember to keep those items needed for your spell readily accessible. Your goddess, god, and quarter candles may all be re-used for the next ritual. We like using full-sized silver and gold taper candles for the goddess and god, respectively, because they will last for a year's worth of rituals. Similarly, because of their glass casing and low burning wax, 7-day votive candles will last for at least a year's worth of rituals as well. They are excellent for use as quarter candles.

Preparation for Spiritual Work and Ritual

We have learned visualization techniques, and now we have the perfect opportunity to apply these principles in attuning our bodies and minds for our sacred rites. We will adapt and integrate the East Indian concept of chakras into our work. In brief, chakras represent energy centers that are theoretically identified along the spine and are essential to life flow energy. For our purposes we will focus on the seven major chakras. However, Anodea Judith's book *Wheels of Life* provides a wonderful understanding of how to identify and work with chakra energy. It is a powerful addition to any library.

The chart provided will outline the color, location, and energy of each chakra and will serve as a handy reference. Keep in mind you have your stone and color correspondences from Chapter 5. For quick reference, I will suggest one stone in the chart as well. That means you can layer your work if you so choose. As you review the chart, imagine seven glowing balls of light at the key centers along your spine.

Energy Chart

Chakra	Color	Location	Energy/Stone
Root	Red	Perineum	Survival/ Red Jasper
Sacral	Orange	Sacrum	Sexual energy/Orange Calcite
Solar plexus	Yellow	Solar plexus	Will/Yellow Aventurine
Heart	Green	Heart	Universal love/Green Aventurine
Throat	Blue	Throat	Speaking truths/Sodalite
Third Eye	Purple	Forehead	Intuition/Amethyst
Crown	White	Crown of head	Spiritual enlightenment/ Moonstone

Prior to every ritual take the time to perform the grounding and centering ritual provided. You can modify it as you become more adept at chakra work, but allow the visualization to serve as the core for opening your chakras. You will find a reminder to close down your chakras from crown to root at the close of each ritual.

The Plane of Vision: A Guide for Opening the Chakras

Ground and Prepare:

See yourself upon the plane of vision. Before you stretches an electric blue horizon. Here, all things are all possible. You exist between worlds and between time. Take a moment to drink in this space. Feel the calm within the energy. (Pause) Now, breathe in silver-light energy. See it fill and energize your body. Exhale any grey negativity. See the grey dissipate into the electric blue horizon. (Allow time for "3" breaths). From your Root Chakra, see a cord extend down into the plane. Through this, you may drink in green, earth energy. Allow the energy to fill your being, grounding you, and connecting you to the sacred plane of earth.

Fill your being with this charge. Allow it to course through your Root Chakra, and then flow into your Sacral Chakra. Feel the energy fill your Solar plexus Chakra, and then embrace your Heart Chakra, warming you. Now, resonate with green, earth energy as it pulses to your Third eye Chakra. As the green, earth energy enters your Crown Chakra, hold it there. Feel yourself alive with and connected to the earth. Now, open the Crown Chakra and allow the white light of the universe to pour into you, mixing and merging with the green, earth energy.

You are alive with the light of the universe and the pulse of the earth. Hold this power. Draw from it as you need to. On this night, for this rite, you hold within you a reserve of earth energy and that of the Universe. Feel your charkas pulse and sing. Breathe deeply and center upon the plane of vision.

***

We must connect to an energy center before beginning ritual. The reasoning is simple. Because we draw upon energy to create circle, we need to enhance our energy stores rather than deplete them. Now that we possess an understanding of the chakras and the importance of grounding, it is time to apply what we've learned through the magic of ritual.

The Rituals

Take the time to read and familiarize yourself with each ritual. Have your consecration and quarter calls written before you begin the rite. Memorization is not necessary, but make sure that you are comfortable with any spoken aspects of ritual. Even if you work alone, you want to feel the flow of the ritual, rather than worry about what to say and how to say it. Ensure that your tools are readily available. You will find the necessary tools outlined from Chapter 4 with some additions listed at the start of each ritual. Any additional tools specific to a given sabbat will appear at the end of the list with an asterisk (*) next to them.

Choose a time when you won't be interrupted and a place, with room to work, where you won't be disturbed. As always, the most important part is your intent. Be cleansed, well rested, and in the proper frame of mind to send and receive the blessings and energy of each sabbat.

Because Imbolc speaks to new hope and the promise of blessings to come, it is an ideal place to begin.

Seeds of Change

An Imbolc Ritual

February 2nd

You will need:

- A work space or altar ideally facing the east or northeast

- (1) White sage bundle

- Frankincense and Myrrh resin with charcoal, or incense sticks

- An abalone shell or ash catcher

- Matches and/or a lighter

- Pen(s) for group work

- Sheets of parchment or lined paper for writing

- (1) Small, white working candle

- (1) White feather (optional)

- (1) Silver candle for Goddess energy

- (1) Gold candle for God energy

- A dish of sea salt

- A dish of spring water

- Representation for the element of air

- Representation for the element of fire

- A drinking chalice or goblet

- A beverage: Select a seasonally appropriate beverage. Wine or juice is fine. For spring and summer, consider white wine or a fruit juice like white grape or apple. For fall and winter, a red wine or grape juice will work nicely.

- Altar cakes. You may bake or purchase your altar cakes. For this ritual, I suggest a sweet corn cake or corn muffins. Make your choice something you feel is appropriate for sharing with and offering to deity.

Optional items:

- Corresponding colored candles and representations for each of the Four Quarters. 7-day devotional candles are recommended.

- Personal tools such as a wand or athame.

- God and goddess figures and/or altar representations

- Altar cloth

- A compass to determine the directions of the Quarters. This is only necessary if, like me, you are directionally impaired.

The Ritual

Ensure that you have placed all of your quarter representations in the appropriate quarter and that all tools are readily available. Have the cakes ready on an altar plate and the beverage poured into the chalice. Take a seat before your altar. Begin by grounding and centering with the chakra visualization. Once you have accomplished this, you are ready to cast circle.

Creating the circle:

- Using the sage, frankincense, and myrrh cast a Pagan Circle as you learned at the conclusion of Chapter 4.

- Once you have cast circle, return to the east. Pick up your representation of air, and hold it above your head. Invite the element and elementals of air to attend.

Use the worksheet provided for your quarter call to the east. Use

extra sheets of paper if needed.

| |
| |
| |
| |
| |
| |

- When you have finished your quarter call, if you have decided to use corresponding quarter candles, you may light the yellow quarter candle now.

- Continue in a clockwise (deosil) direction to the Southern Quarter. Pick up your representation of fire, and hold it aloft. Use the space provided for your quarter call to the south.

- When you have finished your quarter call, if you have decided to use corresponding quarter candles, you may light the red quarter candle now.

Use the space provided for your quarter call to the south.

- Continue in a clockwise direction to the Western Quarter. Pick up

  your representation of water, and hold it aloft.

Use the space provided for your quarter call to the west.

- When you have finished your quarter call, if you have decided to use corresponding quarter candles, you may light the blue quarter candle now.

- Continue in a clockwise direction to the Northern Quarter. Pick up your representation of earth, and hold it aloft.

Use the space provided for your quarter call to the north.

| |
| |
| |
| |
| |
| |
| |

- When you have finished your quarter call, if you have decided to use corresponding quarter candles, you may light the green quarter candle now.

- Continue in a clockwise direction to the Eastern Quarter. Raise your arms in a salute to the east, and then return to your altar.

- **Consecration:** You may use the example provided or write your own.

Awaken from winter's dark night. If we are to plant the seeds of change, then we must lure the light.

- **Bringing power to the circle**

   Stand before your altar. Envision silver-white rays of moonlight
   entering your Crown Chakra as you chant:

   "Silver Lady, Lady Bright, fill me with power and energy this rite.

   Lord of Light, Lord of the Land, let my work be by your hand."

Circle the altar and repeat the chant several times until you feel the energy in the circle increase.

- **Invitation to The God and Goddess**

  "Oak King, whose light is the Sun, I call upon your energy that we may be one. Lady of Fire, Lady of Light, rise, come and be one with _____(circle leader's name) this rite."

- Light the gold candle (god), followed by the silver candle (goddess).

- **The Message**

  We spent the fall in a period of introspection and the winter at rest. Now, we stand restless and ready to feel the warmth and light of The Lord, to tend the earth—our mother—and plant the seeds of planning. In truth, our Lady Mother is not yet ready. She awaits her Lord and his warmth to bring light and life to her womb. As the wheel turns, and the earth awaits, we awaken with much to do. We must cleanse and make ready.

  In times of old, the land was prepared with salt, ashes, and sacred herbs. The Roman Goddess Februa was honored. She was the Goddess of Fresh Starts, and February was known as the cleansing time. We take a lesson from our ancestors and apply it to our times. We are no longer the gatherers, the planters. However, just as in ritual we first cleanse before working magick, we must now ritually and symbolically cleanse our souls and ourselves that we may plant anew.

(Hand out paper/pens if working with a group).

- **The Lesson:**

Imbolc is a time of beginnings, inspiration, and commitment. It is a celebration of possibilities. On a piece of paper, write at least one goal or task that you would like to accomplish during the coming year. Ensure that it is something you feel passionate about doing, beginning, committing to, and/or repairing. Begin your statement with: "I have." In this way you have already begun the positive visualization process. Next, write your plan. For example, I have abundance in my life. I have a loving, nurturing relationship, and so forth.

1. On a separate sheet of paper, for each task or goal you have written, write down the obstacle(s) you feel may hinder your work or commitment. Read the banishing

spell aloud for each obstacle written, ensuring that you name the obstacle at the beginning of the spell.

Banishing Spell

State the Obstacle, I banish you from my life.

No longer will you cause struggle and strife.

This negativity I now release,

that I may sow the seeds of peace.

May my work grant my desire,

by the power of earth, sea, wind, and fire.

2. Next, hold the paper upon which you have written your goal/task. Recite your goal/task aloud, and then repeat this affirmation.

Affirmation

Each day I focus upon my task,

aid from Universe I do ask.

Grant me the tools and that which I need,

Teachings of an Outlaw Witch

so that my goals I will achieve.

By all the power of 3x3,

as I do will, so mote it be!

3. Repeat your goals and the actualizing spell aloud during the waxing to full moon phase of every month until you have achieved your desires. For example, "I have abundance in my life. I have love in my life." Each of these mornings, finish by reciting the actualizing spell aloud.

- **Sharing**

  Take time to feast and enjoy the circle you have cast. Ensure that you leave a sampling of the cakes and a taste of the beverage as an offering.

Closing the Circle

- Give thanks to The Lady and The Lord for their attendance. After thanking each, first snuff The Lord's candle, and then snuff The Lady's candle.

- Stand and move clockwise to the Eastern Quarter. Call to the guardians of the east and recite your quarter closing, offering thanks.

- Upon completion of your quarter closing, snuff the yellow candle and move clockwise (deosil) to the south.

- Standing in the Southern Quarter, call to the guardians of the south and offer your closing and thanks.

| |
| |
| |
| |
| |
| |
| |

- Upon completion of your quarter closing, snuff the red candle and move deosil to the west.

- Standing in the Western Quarter, call to the guardians of the west and thank them.

- Upon completion of your quarter closing, snuff the blue candle and move deosil to the north.

- Standing in the Northern Quarter, call to the guardians of the north and offer your closing and thanks.

| |
| |
| |
| |
| |
| |

- Upon completion of your quarter closing, snuff the green candle and continue moving deosil to your altar.

- **Grounding**

  Take a moment to ground and close your chakras. Working from the Crown Chakra down to the root, envision the balls of light protected and covered.

- **Closing Chant**

  All energies attracted to this rite,

  depart now from this sacred site.

  Upon my will, and the words I have spoken, the circle is open, yet remains unbroken.

  Merry Meet, Merry Part, and Merry Meet again.

- **The Offering**

  Conclude your ritual by setting out the offering and returning your tools to the appropriate place.

Romancing the Shadow

An Ostara Ritual

March 20-21 (Depending upon year)

You will need:

- A work space or altar ideally facing the east or northeast

- (1) White sage bundle

- Frankincense and Myrrh resin with charcoal, or incense sticks

- An abalone shell or ash catcher

- Matches and/or a lighter

- Pen(s) for group work

- Sheets of parchment or lined paper for writing

- (1) Small, white working candle

- (1) White feather (optional)

- (1) Silver candle for Goddess energy

- (1) Gold candle for God energy

- A dish of sea salt

- A dish of spring water

- Representation for the element of air

- Representation for the element of fire

- A drinking chalice or goblet

- An extra drinking glass*

- Select a seasonally appropriate beverage. Wine or juice is fine. For spring and summer, consider white wine or a fruit juice like white grape or apple. For fall and winter, a red wine or grape juice will work nicely.

- Altar cakes: You may bake or purchase your altar cakes. Make your choice something you feel is appropriate for sharing with and offering to deity. I recommend sweet cakes or hot cross buns.

Optional items:

- Corresponding colored candles and representations for each of the Four Quarters. 7-day devotional candles are recommended.

- Personal tools such as a wand or athame.

- God and goddess figures and/or altar representations

- Altar cloth

The Ritual

Ensure that you have placed all of your quarter representations in the appropriate quarter and that all tools are readily available. Have the cakes ready on an altar plate and the beverage poured into the chalice. Take a seat before your altar. Begin by grounding and centering with the chakra visualization. Once you have accomplished this, you are ready to cast circle.

Creating the circle:

- Using the sage, frankincense, and myrrh cast a Pagan Circle as you learned at the conclusion of Chapter 4.

- Once you have cast circle, return to the east. Pick up your representation of air, and hold it above your head. Invite the element and elementals of air to attend. Use the worksheet provided for your quarter call to the east.

Use extra sheets of paper if needed.

| |
| |
| |
| |
| |
| |
| |
| |

- When you have finished your quarter call, if you have decided to use corresponding quarter candles, you may light the yellow quarter candle now.

- Continue in a clockwise (deosil) direction to the Southern Quarter. Pick up your representation of fire, and hold it aloft.

Use the space provided for your quarter call to the south.

| |
| |
| |
| |
| |
| |
| |

- When you have finished your quarter call, if you have decided to use corresponding quarter candles, you may light the red quarter candle now.
- Continue in a clockwise direction to the Western Quarter. Pick up your representation of water, and hold it aloft.

Use the space provided for your quarter call to the west.

_____

_____

_____

_____

_____

_____

_____

_____

- When you have finished your quarter call, if you have decided to use corresponding quarter candles, you may light the blue quarter candle now.

- Continue in a clockwise direction to the Northern Quarter. Pick up your representation of earth, and hold it aloft.

Use the space provided for your quarter call to the north.

| |
| |
| |
| |
| |
| |
| |

- When you have finished your quarter call, if you have decided to use corresponding quarter candles, you may light the green quarter candle now.

- Continue in a clockwise direction to the Eastern Quarter. Raise your arms in a salute to the east, and then return to your altar.

- **Consecration:** You may use the example provided or write your own.

Embrace your shadow-self, and so the mystery shall unfold:

there is light within the darkness, and darkness holds all light.

| |
| |
| |
| |
| |
| |

- **Bringing power to the circle**

    Stand before your altar. Envision silver-white rays of moonlight

    entering your Crown Chakra as you chant:

    "Silver Lady, Lady Bright, fill me with power and energy this rite.

    Lord of Light, Lord of the Land, let my work be by your hand."

    Circle the altar and repeat the chant several times until you feel

    the energy in the circle increase.

- **Invitation to The God and Goddess**

  "Oak King, whose light is the Sun, I call upon your energy that we may be one. Lady of Fire, Lady of Light, rise, come and be one with _____(circle leader's name) this rite."

- Light the gold candle (god), followed by the silver candle (goddess).

- **The Message**

  Ostara represents the Vernal Equinox. It is a time when the energies of light and dark come into balance, yet we move toward the light. This is a time of fertility and promise, of blossoming and awakening. It is a time of attunement and a time to bring the self and soul into balance. How then, do we bring the darkness to light and ever embrace the shadow?

  First, take a moment to consider emotions and aspects of self that you hide from the outside world. Consider emotions such as anger, fear, selfishness, and/or aspects of self such as vanity, hedonism, and materialism. Realize that hiding something from yourself doesn't change the fact that it is a part of you. The goal is to bring your feelings and personality tendencies into balance. Do so by acknowledging, loving, and healing those aspects of self that you are taught to hide.

- **The Lesson:**

From the center of your being, take a deep breath and draw up every shadowed aspect of self, every part of you that you are embarrassed by or feel you need to hide. Draw it up into your mouth and expel it into your glass with one, strong exhale. Allow all tension, negativity, and *dis-ease* to flow from you with this breath. Imagine the glass filled with a muddied stream of emotion. Next, pour a small serving of water into your glass. Add a tiny pinch of salt and stir the mixture counterclockwise as you imagine the muddied stream cleansed by the clear water and purified by the salt.

Take the glass and pass it over your candle flame (3) times as you say:

With earth and water,

fire and air,

a path to wholeness

I now prepare.

Take a sip of water. Envision the cleansed and transformed shadow aspects of self, merging with your being. See the water bring light to the corners of your soul. As you take another sip, imagine a complete integration of shadow and light within you. Finish the glass, and then state:

Shadow and light exist within me.

Each holds a purpose,

and balance holds the key.

- **Sharing**

    Take time to feast and enjoy the circle you have cast. Ensure that you leave a sampling of the cakes and a taste of the beverage as an offering.

Closing the Circle

- Give thanks to The Lady and The Lord for their attendance.

After thanking each, first snuff The Lord's candle, and then snuff

The Lady's candle.

- Stand and move clockwise to the Eastern Quarter. Call to the

guardians of the east and recite your quarter closing, offering

thanks.

- Upon completion of your quarter closing, snuff the yellow candle

and move clockwise (deosil) to the south.

Standing in the Southern Quarter, call to the guardians of the south and offer your closing and thanks.

| |
| |
| |
| |
| |
| |
| |

- Upon completion of your quarter closing, snuff the red candle and move deosil to the west.

- Standing in the Western Quarter, call to the guardians of the west

  and thank them.

| |
| |
| |
| |
| |
| |
| |

- Upon completion of your quarter closing, snuff the blue candle

  and move deosil to the north.

- Standing in the Northern Quarter, call to the guardians of the

  north and offer your closing and thanks.

- Upon completion of your quarter closing, snuff the green candle

  and continue moving deosil to your altar.

- **Grounding**

  Take a moment to ground and close your chakras. Working from

  the Crown Chakra down to the root, envision the balls of light

  protected and covered.

- **Closing Chant**

  All energies attracted to this rite,

  depart now from this sacred site.

  Upon my will, and words I have spoken, the circle is open, yet

  unbroken.

  Merry Meet, Merry Part, and Merry Meet again.

- **The Offering**

  Conclude your ritual by setting out the offering and returning

  your tools to the appropriate place.

Awakening

A Beltane Ritual

May 1

You will need:

♦ A work space or altar ideally facing the east or northeast

♦ (1) White sage bundle

♦ Frankincense and Myrrh resin with charcoal, or incense sticks

♦ An abalone shell or ash catcher

♦ Matches and/or a lighter

♦ Pen(s) for group work

♦ Sheets of parchment or lined paper for writing

♦ (1) Small, white working candle

♦ (1) White feather (optional)

♦ (1) Silver candle for Goddess energy

♦ (1) Gold candle for God energy

♦ A dish of sea salt

♦ A dish of spring water

♦ Representation for the element of air

♦ Representation for the element of fire

- A drinking chalice or goblet

- A beverage: Select a seasonally appropriate beverage. Wine or juice is fine. For spring and summer, consider white wine or a fruit juice like white grape or apple. For fall and winter, a red wine or grape juice will work nicely.

- Altar cakes. You may bake or purchase your altar cakes. Make your choice something you feel is appropriate for sharing with and offering to deity. I recommend indulging in sweet, creamy cakes and pies.

Optional items:

- Corresponding colored candles and representations for each of the Four Quarters. 7-day devotional candles are recommended.

- Personal tools such as a wand or athame.

- God and goddess figures and/or altar representations

- Altar cloth

The Ritual

Ensure that you have placed all of your quarter representations in the appropriate quarter and that all tools are readily available. Have the cakes ready on an altar plate and the beverage poured into the chalice.

Take a seat before your altar. Begin by grounding and centering with the chakra visualization. Once you have accomplished this, you are ready to cast circle.

Creating the circle:

- Using the sage, frankincense, and myrrh, cast a Pagan Circle as you learned at the conclusion of Chapter 4.

- Once you have cast circle, return to the east. Pick up your representation of air, and hold it above your head. Invite the element and elementals of air to attend. Use the worksheet provided for your quarter call to the east.

- When you have finished your quarter call, if you have decided to use corresponding quarter candles, you may light the yellow quarter candle now.

- Continue in a clockwise (deosil) direction to the Southern Quarter. Pick up your representation of fire, and hold it aloft. Use the space provided for your quarter call to the south.

- When you have finished your quarter call, if you have decided to use corresponding quarter candles, you may light the red quarter candle now.

- Continue in a clockwise direction to the Western Quarter. Pick up your representation of water, and hold it aloft. Use the space provided for your quarter call to the west.

- When you have finished your quarter call, if you have decided to use corresponding quarter candles, you may light the blue quarter candle now.

- Continue in a clockwise direction to the Northern Quarter. Pick up your representation of earth, and hold it aloft. Use the space provided for your quarter call to the north.

| |
| |
| |
| |
| |
| |
| |

- When you have finished your quarter call, if you have decided to use corresponding quarter candles, you may light the green quarter candle now.

- Continue in a clockwise direction to the Eastern Quarter. Raise your arms in a salute to the east, and then return to your altar.

- **Consecration:** You may use the example provided or write your own.

There is a stirring, an awakening within and without. On this night we conjure summer. As we draw in the promise of warmth, we awaken to ourselves.

- **Bringing power to the circle**

  Stand before your altar. Envision silver-white rays of moonlight entering your Crown Chakra as you chant:

  "Silver Lady, Lady Bright, fill me with power and energy this rite. Lord of Light, Lord of the Land, let my work be by your hand."

  Circle the altar and repeat the chant several times until you feel the energy in the circle increase.

- **Invitation to The God and Goddess**

  "Lord of the Forest, God of the Green, from the blossoming earth your love is seen. Cernnunos, Bacchus, Pan, and Bal—Gods of bounty and pleasure—hear my call. Venus, Aphrodite, sweet keepers of love, I draw your energy from above. Lakshmi, Yemaya, Asherah, All, may your light upon this circle fall.

- Light the gold candle (god), followed by the silver candle (goddess).

- **The Message**

  Bounty, sensuality, fertility: This I am, this I offer. You who know me both within and without, these are your rites and your gifts.

As I join with my Lord and Love, there is no shame in our union. All acts of pleasure are my rites. This most basic and life sustaining act has been defiled in present times. I invite you to rediscover yourselves. Awaken to the life that pulses within you. Take the time to explore what pleases you—and should you share a love, take the time to fathom their needs as well. Know your history and from whence you came. The wheel is but one aspect, and we must be in accordance with all aspects. You come from the mother, whose womb has been given life by the light and love of the god. He, who brings life to the earth, brings life to you and lives within you. She who is life and bounty dwells within you as well. Find their union within your sacred and sacral chakra. Step away from the constraints of society and reach back into the earth—the earth mother. Find the seat of your soul. Explore the mystery within and express it in love without.

- **The Lesson:**

We honor the marriage of our Lady and Lord. How blessed are we to share in this sacred rite. Know that on Beltane, the Lady and Lord exchange their vows to one another and to the children of earth. They vow to nurture and to support, to give and to grow in love. They provide us with the best of themselves. We must awaken these gifts within ourselves. As above, so below. How will you mirror the gifts of The Lady and The Lord? How will you awaken the bounty within? Pledge a vow to your faith and yourself.

- **Sharing**

  Take time to feast and enjoy the circle you have cast. Ensure that you leave a sampling of the cakes and a taste of the beverage as an offering.

Closing the Circle

- Give thanks to The Lady and The Lord for their attendance. After thanking each, first snuff The Lord's candle, and then snuff The Lady's candle.
- Stand and move clockwise to the Eastern Quarter. Call to the guardians of the east and recite your quarter closing, offering thanks.

Use the space provided.

<table>
<tr><td></td></tr>
<tr><td></td></tr>
<tr><td></td></tr>
<tr><td></td></tr>
<tr><td></td></tr>
<tr><td></td></tr>
<tr><td></td></tr>
</table>

- Upon completion of your quarter closing, snuff the yellow candle and move clockwise (deosil) to the south.

- Standing in the Southern Quarter, call to the guardians of the south and offer your closing and thanks.

Use the space provided.

| |
| |
| |
| |
| |
| |

- Upon completion of your quarter closing, snuff the red candle and move deosil to the west.

- Standing in the Western Quarter, call to the guardians of the west and thank them.

Use the space provided.

- Upon completion of your quarter closing, snuff the blue candle and move deosil to the north.

- Standing in the Northern Quarter, call to the guardians of the north and offer your closing and thanks.

Use the space provided.

<table>
<tr><td></td></tr>
<tr><td></td></tr>
<tr><td></td></tr>
<tr><td></td></tr>
<tr><td></td></tr>
<tr><td></td></tr>
<tr><td></td></tr>
<tr><td></td></tr>
</table>

- Upon completion of your quarter closing, snuff the green candle and continue moving deosil to your altar.

- **Grounding**

  Take a moment to ground and close your chakras. Working from the Crown Chakra down to the root, envision the balls of light protected and covered.

- **Closing Chant**

  All energies attracted to this rite,

  depart now from this sacred site.

  Upon my will, and the words I have spoken, the circle is open, yet

  remains unbroken.

  Merry Meet, Merry Part, and Merry Meet again.

- **The Offering**

  Conclude your ritual by setting out the offering and returning

  your tools to the appropriate place.

The Blessing Bowl

A Litha Ritual

June 20-21 (Depending upon year)

You will need:

- A work space or altar ideally facing the east or northeast

- (1) White sage bundle

- Frankincense and Myrrh resin with charcoal, or incense sticks

- An abalone shell or ash catcher

- Matches and/or a lighter

- Pen(s) for group work

- Sheets of parchment or lined paper for writing

- (1) Small, white working candle

- (1) White feather (optional)

- (1) Silver candle for Goddess energy

- (1) Gold candle for God energy

- A dish of sea salt

- A dish of spring water

- Representation for the element of air

- Representation for the element of fire

- A drinking chalice or goblet

- An empty glass jar or dish*

- A beverage: Select a seasonally appropriate beverage. Wine or juice is fine. For spring and summer, consider white wine or a fruit juice like white grape or apple. For fall and winter, a red wine or grape juice will work nicely.

- Altar cakes. You may bake or purchase your altar cakes. Make your choice something you feel is appropriate for sharing with and offering to deity. I recommend cakes and breads with seasonal berries.

Optional items:

♦ Corresponding colored candles and representations for each of the Four Quarters. 7-day devotional candles are recommended.

♦ Personal tools such as a wand or athame.

♦ God and goddess figures and/or altar representations

♦ Altar cloth

The Ritual

Ensure that you have placed all of your quarter representations in the appropriate quarter and that all tools are readily available. Have the cakes ready on an altar plate and the beverage poured into the chalice. Take a seat before your altar. Begin by grounding and centering with the chakra visualization. Once you have accomplished this, you are ready to cast circle.

Creating the circle:

• Using the sage, frankincense, and myrrh, cast a Pagan Circle as you learned at the conclusion of Chapter 4.

- Once you have cast circle, return to the east. Pick up your representation of air, and hold it above your head. Invite the element and elementals of air to attend. Use the worksheet provided for your quarter call to the east. Use extra sheets of paper if needed.

- When you have finished your quarter call, if you have decided to use corresponding quarter candles, you may light the yellow quarter candle now.

- Continue in a clockwise direction to the Southern Quarter. Pick up your representation of fire, and hold it aloft. Use the space provided for your quarter call to the south.

- When you have finished your quarter call, if you have decided to use corresponding quarter candles, you may light the red quarter candle now.

- Continue in a clockwise direction to the Western Quarter. Pick up your representation of water, and hold it aloft. Use the space provided for your quarter call to the west.

- When you have finished your quarter call, if you have decided to use corresponding quarter candles, you may light the blue quarter candle now.

- Continue in a clockwise direction to the Northern Quarter. Pick up your representation of earth, and hold it aloft. Use the space provided for your quarter call to the north.

- When you have finished your quarter call, if you have decided to use corresponding quarter candles, you may light the green quarter candle now.

- Continue in a clockwise direction to the Eastern Quarter. Raise your arms in a salute to the east, and then return to your altar.

- **Consecration:** You may use the example provided or write your own.

> *The Summer Solstice is a time of gathering. Long ago we gathered herbs for healing from the land, our bounty meant to see us through the trials of winter. On this day, we gather our blessings and the tools we will need to see us through challenging times.*

- **Bringing power to the circle**

  Stand before your altar. Envision silver-white rays of moonlight entering your Crown Chakra as you chant:

"Silver Lady, Lady Bright, fill me with power and energy this rite.

Lord of Light, Lord of the Land, let my work be by your hand."

Circle the altar and repeat the chant several times until you feel

the energy in the circle increase.

- **Invitation to The God and Goddess**

  "Lady of the Meadow, Lord of the Land, you hold our blessings

  within your hands. May we know your gifts of light as we gather

  for this rite.

- Light the gold candle (god), followed by the silver candle

  (goddess).

- **The Message**

  We celebrate the earth, and her bounty, soon to be harvested.

  We celebrate the change of season as the Holly King hands over

  his reign to that of his brother, The Oak King. We celebrate nature

  and nurture, even as we recognize our entry into the waning time

  of year. We look to protect the coming gifts and blessings with an

  eye toward the season's change. It is a time of celebration and of

  preparation. Nature's gifts surround us, and we gather summer

  fruits and herbs as we can. Yet, we also prepare ourselves for the season's change by gathering our store of the blessings that will

serve us through the dark time of the year.

- **The Lesson:**

Make a list of what you have been blessed with in life. Nothing is

too simple. Consider your accomplishments and anything that

brings you happiness, or allows you to be present in this life. The

ability to awaken to see a new day is as much a blessing as having

a loving family, a pet, or a life situation that pleases you. Anything

that allows you to *be* is a blessing.

1. Write your blessings on slips of parchment paper. If you
    are feeling creative, you can transfer what you have
    written onto brightly colored construction paper.

2. Gather the slips in your hands, or place your hands over
    them and bless them with your own energy. Envision
    waves of healing, blue energy and streaks of yellow light
    flowing from your hands into the slips of paper. When
    you feel as though you have charged them, ask The
    Lady and Lord to bless and guard these gifts as well.
    Offer them up to the east and give thanks to The Lady,

The Lord, and all good elements and elementals for the bounty and blessings you hold within your hands.

3. Store them in an empty glass jar or a ceramic serving dish. If you like, you can shop around for a decorative box or dish to store your blessings.

4. Throughout the year, whenever you feel blue, or simply need a reminder, reach into the jar and draw one of your blessings. You can even keep the dish by your front door and select one each day upon leaving or returning to your home.

*   **Sharing**

Take time to feast and enjoy the circle you have cast. Ensure that you leave a sampling of the cakes and a taste of the beverage as an offering.

Closing the Circle

*   Give thanks to The Lady and The Lord for their attendance. After thanking each, first snuff The Lord's candle, and then snuff The Lady's candle.

- Stand and move clockwise to the Eastern Quarter. Call to the guardians of the east and recite your quarter closing, offering thanks.

- Upon completion of your quarter closing, snuff the yellow candle and move clockwise (deosil) to the south.
- Standing in the Southern Quarter, call to the guardians of the south and offer your closing and thanks.

Use the space provided.

| |
| |
| |
| |
| |
| |
| |
| |

- Upon completion of your quarter closing, snuff the red candle and move deosil to the west.

- Standing in the Western Quarter, call to the guardians of the west and thank them.

Use the space provided.

<table>
<tr><td></td></tr>
</table>

- Upon completion of your quarter closing, snuff the blue candle and move deosil to the north.

- Standing in the Northern Quarter, call to the guardians of the north and offer your closing and thanks.

Use the space provided.

| |
| |
| |
| |
| |
| |
| |
| |

- Upon completion of your quarter closing, snuff the green candle and continue moving deosil to your altar.

- **Grounding**

- Take a moment to ground and close your chakras. Working from the Crown Chakra down to the root, envision the balls of light protected and covered.

- **Closing Chant**

  All energies attracted to this rite,

  depart now from this sacred site.

  Upon my will, and the words I have spoken, the circle is open, yet

  remains unbroken.

  Merry Meet, Merry Part, and Merry Meet again.

- **The Offering**

  Conclude your ritual by setting out the offering and returning

  your tools to the appropriate place.

The First Harvest

A Lughnasadh Ritual

August 1st

You will need:

- ◆ A work space or altar ideally facing the east or northeast

- ◆ (1) White sage bundle

- ◆ Frankincense and Myrrh resin with charcoal, or incense sticks

- ◆ An abalone shell or ash catcher

- Matches and/or a lighter

- Pen(s) for group work

- Sheets of parchment or lined paper for writing

- (1) Small, white working candle

- (1) White feather (optional)

- (1) Silver candle for Goddess energy

- (1) Gold candle for God energy

- A dish of sea salt

- A dish of spring water

- Representation for the element of air

- Representation for the element of fire

- A drinking chalice or goblet

- A beverage: Select a seasonally appropriate beverage. Wine or juice is fine. For spring and summer, consider white wine or a fruit juice like white grape or apple. For fall and winter, a red wine or grape juice will work nicely.

- Altar cakes. You may bake or purchase your altar cakes. Make your choice something you feel is appropriate for sharing with and offering to deity. I recommend breads and biscuits.

Optional items:

♦ Corresponding colored candles and representations for each of the Four Quarters. 7-day devotional candles are recommended.

♦ Personal tools such as a wand or athame.

♦ God and goddess figures and/or altar representations

♦ Altar cloth

The Ritual

Ensure that you have placed all of your quarter representations in the appropriate quarter, and that all tools are readily available. Have the cakes ready on an altar plate and the beverage poured into the chalice. Take a seat before your altar. Begin by grounding and centering with the chakra visualization. Once you have accomplished this, you are ready to cast circle.

Creating the circle:

• Using the sage, frankincense, and myrrh, cast a Pagan Circle as you learned at the conclusion of Chapter 4.

• Once you have cast circle, return to the east. Pick up your representation of air, and hold it above your head. Invite the element and elementals of air to attend.

Use the worksheet provided for your quarter call to the east.

- When you have finished your quarter call, if you have decided to use corresponding quarter candles, you may light the yellow quarter candle now.

- Continue in a clockwise (deosil) direction to the Southern Quarter. Pick up your representation of fire, and hold it aloft.

Use the space provided for your quarter call to the south.

- When you have finished your quarter call, if you have decided to use corresponding quarter candles, you may light the red quarter candle now.

- Continue in a clockwise direction to the Western Quarter. Pick up your representation of water, and hold it aloft.

Use the space provided for your quarter call to the west.

- When you have finished your quarter call, if you have decided to use corresponding quarter candles, you may light the blue quarter candle now.

- Continue in a clockwise direction to the Northern Quarter. Pick up your representation of earth, and hold it aloft.

Use the space provided for your quarter call to the north.

- When you have finished your quarter call, if you have decided to use corresponding quarter candles, you may light the green quarter candle now.

- Continue in a clockwise direction to the Eastern Quarter. Raise your arms in a salute to the east, and then return to your altar.

- **Consecration:** You may use the example provided or write your

  own.

On Lughnasadh, a solar festival, we celebrate the First Harvest.

Here, we gather the budding bounty of our labors.

- **Bringing power to the circle**

  Stand before your altar. Envision silver-white rays of moonlight

  entering your Crown Chakra as you chant:

  "Silver Lady, Lady Bright, fill me with power and energy this rite.

Dark Lord, mighty protector of the Land, let my work be by your

hand."

Circle the altar and repeat the chant several times until you feel

the energy in the circle increase.

- **Invitation to The God and Goddess**

  "To you we call, Dark Lord of gift and sacrifice, and our Lady of

  light and the sacred night, please join us now in this blessed rite.

- Light the gold candle (god), followed by the silver candle

  (goddess).

- **The Message**

  Lughnasadh is a solar festival. It celebrates the Celtic god, Lugh, of

  the Tuatha De Danann—an ancient race of gods—as well as his

  creation of the funeral games in homage to his foster mother—

  Tailtiu—the last queen of the Fir Bolg. The sacred myth states that

  she died after clearing a great forest so that the land could be

  cultivated. Lughnasadh celebrates not only the sacrifice of the

  Lord, who turned himself into a sheaf of wheat to feed the

  children of Earth, but the mother—great goddess of agriculture—

  without whom there would be no harvest. In our celebration, we honor the interplay of light and dark, of sacrifice and gift, sun and earth, mother and father. How blessed are we the children of the Ancient and Shining Ones.

- **The Lesson:**

The Dark Lord, lord of gift and sacrifice, holds the fire and light of life within. It is your divine spark and the spark of life within you. It is your creativity and passion. How will you honor and feed the fire? How will you use your divine light to foster change in the world?

1. Begin by thinking of the blessings you listed for Litha, or any blessing that has graced your life. It doesn't have to be anything complex, but the idea is to think of a gift or talent that you have been blessed with that you can share with the world.

2. Once you have decided on a talent, blessing, or kindness that has made a difference in your life, devise a way to pay that kindness forward. It can be as simple as giving your seat to an elderly person on the bus, or donating cans of food. Perhaps you can adopt a pet, or

donate your time to a worthy cause. Maybe you have a message to share, or know of someone who could use a helping hand.

Your lesson is to look for a means of stoking the fire of light and creativity within you, and then sharing that spark and blessing with the world, even if that begins with only one person. We must be the change we wish to see in the world, but we must also share that energy in order to create change.

- **Sharing**

  Take time to feast and enjoy the circle you have cast. Ensure that you leave a sampling of the cakes and a taste of the beverage as an offering.

Closing the Circle

- Give thanks to The Lady and The Lord for their attendance. After thanking each, first snuff The Lord's candle, and then snuff The Lady's candle.

- Stand and move clockwise to the Eastern Quarter. Call to the guardians of the east and recite your quarter closing, offering thanks.

- Upon completion of your quarter closing, snuff the yellow candle and move clockwise (deosil) to the south.
- Standing in the Southern Quarter, call to the guardians of the south and offer your closing thanks.

Use the space provided.

- Upon completion of your quarter closing, snuff the red candle and move deosil to the west.

- Standing in the Western Quarter, call to the guardians of the west and thank them.

Use the space provided.

| |
| |
| |
| |
| |
| |
| |

- Upon completion of your quarter closing, snuff the blue candle and move deosil to the north.

- Standing in the Northern Quarter, call to the guardians of the north and offer your closing and thanks.

Use the space provided.

<table>
<tr><td></td></tr>
<tr><td></td></tr>
<tr><td></td></tr>
<tr><td></td></tr>
<tr><td></td></tr>
<tr><td></td></tr>
<tr><td></td></tr>
</table>

- Upon completion of your quarter closing, snuff the green candle and continue moving deosil to your altar.

- **Grounding**

  Take a moment to ground and close your chakras. Working from the Crown Chakra down to the root, envision the balls of light protected and covered.

- **Closing Chant**

  All energies attracted to this rite,

  depart now from this sacred site.

  Upon my will, and the words I have spoken, the circle is open, yet

  remains unbroken.

  Merry Meet, Merry Part, and Merry Meet again.

- **The Offering**

  Conclude your ritual by setting out the offering and returning

  your tools to the appropriate place.

Holding the Flame Within

A Mabon Ritual

September 21-22nd (Depending upon year)

You will need:

♦ A work space or altar ideally facing the east or northeast

♦ (1) White sage bundle

♦ Frankincense and Myrrh resin with charcoal, or incense sticks

♦ An abalone shell or ash catcher

- Matches and/or a lighter

- Pen(s) for group work

- Sheets of parchment or lined paper for writing

- (1) Small, white working candle

- (1) White feather (optional)

- (1) Silver candle for Goddess energy

- (1) Gold candle for God energy

- A dish of sea salt

- A dish of spring water

- Representation for the element of air

- Representation for the element of fire

- A drinking chalice or goblet

- (1) Black Candle (a small chime candle is fine)*

- (1) White Candle (a small chime candle is fine)*

- A beverage: Select a seasonally appropriate beverage. Wine or juice is fine. For spring and summer, consider white wine or a fruit juice like white grape or apple. For fall and winter, a red wine or grape juice will work nicely.

♦ Altar cakes. You may bake or purchase your altar cakes. Make your choice something you feel is appropriate for sharing with and offering to deity. I recommend a rich banana bread.

Optional items:

♦ Corresponding colored candles and representations for each of the Four Quarters. 7-day devotional candles are recommended.

♦ Personal tools such as a wand or athame.

♦ God and goddess figures and/or altar representations

♦ Altar cloth

The Ritual

Ensure that you have placed all of your quarter representations in the appropriate quarter, and that all tools are readily available. Have the cakes ready on an altar plate and the beverage poured into the chalice. Take a seat before your altar. Begin by grounding and centering with the chakra visualization. Once you have accomplished this, you are ready to cast circle.

Creating the circle:

• Using the sage, frankincense, and myrrh, cast a Pagan Circle as you learned at the conclusion of Chapter 4.

- Once you have cast circle, return to the east. Pick up your representation of air, and hold it above your head. Invite the element and elementals of air to attend. Use the worksheet provided for your quarter call to the east. Use extra sheets of paper if needed.

- When you have finished your quarter call, if you have decided to use corresponding quarter candles, you may light the yellow quarter candle now.

- Continue in a clockwise (deosil) direction to the Southern Quarter. Pick up your representation of fire, and hold it aloft. Use the space provided for your quarter call to the south.

- When you have finished your quarter call, if you have decided to use corresponding quarter candles, you may light the red quarter candle now.

- Continue in a clockwise direction to the Western Quarter. Pick up your representation of water, and hold it aloft. Use the space provided for your quarter call to the west.

- When you have finished your quarter call, if you have decided to use corresponding quarter candles, you may light the blue quarter candle now.

- Continue in a clockwise direction to the Northern Quarter. Pick up your representation of earth, and hold it aloft. Use the space provided for your quarter call to the north.

- When you have finished your quarter call, if you have decided to use corresponding quarter candles, you may light the green quarter candle now.

- Continue in a clockwise direction to the Eastern Quarter. Raise your arms in a salute to the east, and then return to your altar.

- **Consecration:** You may use the example provided or write your own.

We circle 'round to hold the flame. With our light we embrace the darkness. For, the shadow is of the self as much as the light is of the soul.

- **Bringing power to the circle**

   Stand before your altar. Envision silver-white rays of moonlight entering your Crown Chakra as you chant:

"Silver Lady, Lady Bright, fill me with power and energy this rite.

Dark Lord, mighty protector of the Land, let my work be by your

hand."

Circle the altar and repeat the chant several times until you feel

the energy in the circle increase.

- **Invitation to The God and Goddess**

   "To you we call, Dark Lord of gift and sacrifice, and our Lady of

   light and the sacred night, please join us now in this blessed rite.

- Light the gold candle (god), followed by the silver candle

   (goddess).

- **The Message**

   The energy of this time is deeper, subtle, and resonates with the

   underworld deities. Hecate, Persephone, Kali, Inana, Legba,

   Anubis, Shiva. Our focus is to work toward the acceptance and

   integration of our shadow, bringing the energies of light and

   darkness to balance within, realizing that our shadow is

   responsible for the light. Therefore, we light a flame for ourselves

   as we embrace the darkness. We must look deeper into our

   intuitive senses and honor these gifts.

- **The Lesson:**

Ensure that all chakras are open.

1. Light the black candle and meditate upon shadow. Who are the Crones and Dark Lords of the shadows? What gifts and wisdom do they bring? Kali, Goddess of Time, Death, and Rebirth. Shiva, Lord of Wisdom. Cerridwen, Keeper of the Cauldron of Rebirth. Hecate and Legba Keepers of the Crossroads, link between worlds. Anubis, Lord of the Underworld. All represent timelessness, power, knowledge, wisdom, and life beyond the confines of death. They move seamlessly behind the veil, balancing darkness and light, life and death, creation and destruction.

2. Consider the ways in which we misuse the gifts of the shadows. When we see our own shadow-self, do we rise into the light or settle into the depths of darkness? How can we bring shadow into balance with light?

3. Take a minute to meditate on the deities and blessings of the darkness. Ask for their wisdom.

4. See the shadow-self integrated within you. Its emotions are a part of your being. However, emotions do not rule you. At all times you choose whether or not you will react to, express, or expose their energies.

5. Gaze upon the black candle's flame and state: I accept that I come from darkness into the light. I embrace the roots of darkness. I embrace the branches of light. Let me not be ruled by either, but be in balance with the energies that are all that I am.

6. Light the white candle and state: I hold light within the darkness. As Yin is to Yang, I am balanced, a candle within the cauldron of my being.

- **Sharing**

Take time to feast and enjoy the circle you have cast. Ensure that you leave a sampling of the cakes and a taste of the beverage as an offering.

Closing the Circle

- Give thanks to The Lady and The Lord for their attendance. After thanking each, first snuff The Lord's candle, and then snuff The Lady's candle.

- Stand and move clockwise to the Eastern Quarter. Call to the guardians of the East and recite your quarter closing, offering thanks.

<table>
<tr><td></td></tr>
<tr><td></td></tr>
<tr><td></td></tr>
<tr><td></td></tr>
<tr><td></td></tr>
<tr><td></td></tr>
<tr><td></td></tr>
</table>

- Upon completion of your quarter closing, snuff the yellow candle and move clockwise (deosil) to the south.
- Standing in the Southern Quarter, call to the guardians of the south and offer your closing and thanks.

Use the space provided.

| |
| |
| |
| |
| |
| |
| |

- Upon completion of your quarter closing, snuff the red candle and move deosil to the west.

- Standing in the Western Quarter, call to the guardians of the west and thank them.

Use the space provided.

| |
| |
| |
| |
| |
| |
| |
| |

- Upon completion of your quarter closing, snuff the blue candle and move deosil to the north.

- Standing in the Northern Quarter, call to the guardians of the north and offer your closing and thanks.

Use the space provided.

| |
| |
| |
| |
| |
| |
| |

- Upon completion of your quarter closing, snuff the green candle and continue moving deosil to your altar.

- **Grounding**

  Take a moment to ground and close your chakras. Working from the Crown Chakra down to the root, envision the balls of light protected and covered.

- **Closing chant**

  All energies attracted to this rite,

  depart now from this sacred site.

  Upon my will, and the words I have spoken, the circle is open, yet remains unbroken.

  Merry Meet, Merry Part, and Merry Meet again.

- **The Offering**

  Conclude your ritual by setting out the offering and returning your tools to the appropriate place.

Teachings of the Crone

Balance Between Light and Dark/Life and Death

A Samhain Ritual

October 31st

You will need:

- ◆ A work space or altar ideally facing the east or northeast
- ◆ (1) White sage bundle
- ◆ Frankincense and Myrrh resin with charcoal, or incense sticks

- An abalone shell or ash catcher

- Matches and/or a lighter

- Pen(s) for group work

- Sheets of parchment or lined paper for writing

- (1) Small, white working candle

- (1) White feather (optional)

- (1) Silver candle for Goddess energy

- (1) Gold candle for God energy

- A dish of sea salt

- A dish of spring water

- Representation for the element of air

- Representation for the element of fire

- A drinking chalice or goblet

- (1) Black Candle (a small chime candle is fine)*

- A heat resistant container for burning*

- A beverage: Select a seasonally appropriate beverage. Wine or juice is fine. For spring and summer, consider white wine or a fruit juice like white grape or apple. For fall and winter, a red wine or grape juice will work nicely.

♦ Altar cakes. You may bake or purchase your altar cakes. Make
  your choice something you feel is appropriate for sharing with
  and offering to deity. I recommend apple and pumpkin pies.

Optional items:

♦ Corresponding colored candles and representations for each of
  the Four Quarters. 7-day devotional candles are recommended.

♦ Personal tools such as a wand or athame.

♦ God and goddess figures and/or altar representations

♦ Altar cloth

The Ritual

Ensure that you have placed all of your quarter representations in
the appropriate quarter, and that all tools are readily available. Have
the cakes ready on an altar plate and the beverage poured into the
chalice. Take a seat before your altar. Begin by grounding and centering
with the chakra visualization. Once you have accomplished this, you are
ready to cast circle.

Creating the circle:

- Using the sage, frankincense, and myrrh, cast a Pagan Circle as you learned at the conclusion of Chapter 4.

- Once you have cast circle, return to the east. Pick up your representation of air, and hold it above your head. Invite the element and elementals of air to attend. Use the worksheet provided for your quarter call to the east. Use extra sheets of paper if needed.

- When you have finished your quarter call, if you have decided to use corresponding quarter candles, you may light the yellow quarter candle now.

- Continue in a clockwise (deosil) direction to the Southern Quarter. Pick up your representation of fire, and hold it aloft. Use the space provided for your quarter call to the south.

| |
| |
| |
| |
| |
| |
| |

- When you have finished your quarter call, if you have decided to use corresponding quarter candles, you may light the red quarter candle now.

- Continue in a clockwise direction to the Western Quarter. Pick up your representation of water, and hold it aloft. Use the space provided for your quarter call to the west.

- When you have finished your quarter call, if you have decided to use corresponding quarter candles, you may light the blue quarter candle now.

- Continue in a clockwise direction to the Northern Quarter. Pick up your representation of earth, and hold it aloft. Use the space provided for your quarter call to the north.

- When you have finished your quarter call, if you have decided to use corresponding quarter candles, you may light the green quarter candle now.

- Continue in a clockwise direction to the Eastern Quarter. Raise your arms in a salute to the east, and then return to your altar.

- **Consecration:** You may use the example provided or write your own.

I am the Crone Goddess, Dark Mother, White Lady. Before me is my cauldron of Death and Rebirth. All will come to me—all will come through me. What will be is, and what once was will be again. This is the cycle and the way.

- **Bringing power to the circle**

  Stand before your altar. Envision silver-white rays of moonlight entering your Crown Chakra as you chant:

  "Lady Light, Lady Night, fill me with power and energy this rite. Lord of Sacrifice Lord of the Land, let my work be by your hand."

  Circle the altar and repeat the chant several times until you feel the energy in the circle increase.

- **Invitation to The God and Goddess**

  "Dark Lord, Dark Mother. Holly King, Holy Hunter. Lady of White, Mother of Old and All. I call to you this night. Rise; come and be one with your witch, (insert circle leader's name), this rite.

- Light the gold candle (god), followed by the silver candle (goddess).

- **The Message**

  I speak to you as Crone. Through time and cultures you have known me as Cerridwen, Kali, Oya, and the many names of my sisters through turns and ages. My face is that of darkness, yet look closer and see light within the shadow, life beyond death.

On this night, though my Lord passes through to the Summerland, he will take my burden and my reign. As he is transformed, so shall I be, for all is but a turn of the wheel.

You, children of divine union, come before me. You shall give to me that which is your burden, that which must die, and from me take a gift in return. Know that in death there is life. Never shall you hunger, nor thirst, nor know of void as long as you know the mystery and the way. Where you find me, you find life. In all aspects: as above, so below, as within, so without. Children, if you seek that which is truly divine, then know this and heed me well: Before time and ages, I scattered my Lord and Love into the cosmic winds. I sent him to find Himself, and to find me. How will he know himself? How will he find me? *As within, so without.* You, who are seekers, find yourselves. Find The Divine.

- **The Lesson:**

As we move into the witches' New Year, find the quiet space within your soul to reflect upon what you have reaped these past few months. Have the seeds that you have planted and the plans that you have nurtured flourished and sustained you? At this, the final harvest, what will you tend? What must be sacrificed? Look deep within and provide an honest assessment of the year and of yourself. Remember, for all that we release, we must replenish.

Do the following:

1. Light the black candle. Take a moment to gaze at the flame. Allow yourself to relax.

2. Consider what you will cast to the fire, and what will rise from the flame to take its place.

3. Use the parchment paper to write what you wish to release. Once you have written what you will release, burn it in the heat resistant container. Use the imagery of the crone's cauldron. All that is cast into the cauldron and to the flame is transformed and reborn.

4. Next, write down what will rise from the flame to take its place. This is the energy, purpose, or plan you will adopt to replace what you have released. For example, if you have released a plan for getting a new job because it didn't work out, perhaps you will replace that

with acquiring new or necessary skills to obtain your

goal.

5. Lastly, spend time reflecting on the year and the

wisdom and lessons of the crone. Realize that you have

cast your burden to her, so that she may help you

transform your life and your plans. Her gift is that of

renewal. Apply her teachings to bring wholeness and

change to your life.

- **Sharing**

Take time to feast and enjoy the circle you have cast. Ensure that

you leave a sampling of the cakes and a taste of the beverage as

an offering.

Closing the Circle

- Give thanks to The Lady and The Lord for their attendance. After

thanking each, first snuff The Lord's candle, and then snuff The

Lady's candle.

- Stand and move clockwise to the Eastern Quarter. Call to the

guardians of the east and recite your quarter closing, offering

thanks.

Use the space provided.

- Upon completion of your quarter closing, snuff the yellow candle and move clockwise (deosil) to the south.

- Standing in the Southern Quarter, call to the guardians of the south and offer your closing and thanks.

Use the space provided.

- Upon completion of your quarter closing, snuff the red candle and move deosil to the west.

- Standing in the Western Quarter, call to the guardians of the west and thank them.

Use the space provided.

- Upon completion of your quarter closing, snuff the blue candle and move deosil to the north.

- Standing in the Northern Quarter, call to the guardians of the north and offer your closing and thanks.

Use the space provided.

- Upon completion of your quarter closing, snuff the green candle and continue moving deosil to your altar.

- ***For this sabbat only, make one pass around the altar counter-clockwise (widdershins) if you feel there is any energy that you would further like to release or undo.**

- **Grounding**

  Take a moment to ground and close your chakras.

Working from the Crown Chakra down to the root, envision the balls of light protected and covered.

- **Closing Chant**

All energies attracted to this rite,

depart now from this sacred site.

Upon my will, and the words I have spoken, the circle is open, yet remains unbroken.

Merry Meet, Merry Part, and Merry Meet again.

- **The Offering**

Conclude your ritual by setting out the offering and returning your tools to the appropriate place.

The Promise of Light

A Yule Ritual

December 21-22nd (Depending on year)

You will need:

- A work space or altar ideally facing the east or northeast
- (1) White sage bundle

- Frankincense and Myrrh resin with charcoal, or incense sticks

- An abalone shell or ash catcher

- Matches and/or a lighter

- Pen(s) for group work

- Sheets of parchment or lined paper for writing

- (1) Small, white working candle

- (1) White feather (optional)

- (1) Silver candle for Goddess energy

- (1) Gold candle for God energy

- A dish of sea salt

- A dish of spring water

- Representation for the element of air

- Representation for the element of fire

- A drinking chalice or goblet

- (1) Black Candle (a small chime candle is fine)*

- (1) Red Candle (a small chime candle is fine)*

- (1) White Candle (a small chime candle is fine)*

- (1) Green Candle(a small chime candle is fine)*

- A beverage: Select a seasonally appropriate beverage. Wine or juice is fine. For spring and summer, consider white wine or a fruit juice like white grape or apple. For fall and winter, a red wine or grape juice will work nicely.

♦ Altar cakes. You may bake or purchase your altar cakes. Make your choice something you feel is appropriate for sharing with and offering to deity. I recommend rich chocolate or gingerbread cakes.

Optional items:

♦ Corresponding colored candles and representations for each of the Four Quarters. 7-day devotional candles are recommended.

♦ Personal tools such as a wand or athame.

♦ God and goddess figures and/or altar representations

♦ Altar cloth

The Ritual

Ensure that you have placed all of your quarter representations in the appropriate quarter, and that all tools are readily available. Have the cakes ready on an altar plate and the beverage poured into the chalice. Take a seat before your altar. Begin by grounding and centering with the chakra visualization. Once you have accomplished this, you are ready to cast circle.

Creating the circle:

- Using the sage, frankincense, and myrrh, cast a Pagan Circle as you learned at the conclusion of Chapter 4.

- Once you have cast circle, return to the east. Pick up your representation of air, and hold it above your head. Invite the element and elementals of air to attend. Use the worksheet provided for your quarter call to the east. Use extra sheets of paper if needed.

| |
| |
| |
| |
| |
| |
| |

- When you have finished your quarter call, if you have decided to use corresponding quarter candles, you may light the yellow quarter candle now.

- Continue in a clockwise (deosil) direction to the Southern Quarter. Pick up your representation of fire, and hold it aloft. Use the space provided for your quarter call to the south.

- When you have finished your quarter call, if you have decided to use corresponding quarter candles, you may light the red quarter candle now.

- Continue in a clockwise direction to the Western Quarter. Pick up your representation of water, and hold it aloft. Use the space provided for your quarter call to the west.

- When you have finished your quarter call, if you have decided to use corresponding quarter candles, you may light the blue quarter candle now.

- Continue in a clockwise direction to the Northern Quarter. Pick up your representation of earth, and hold it aloft. Use the space provided for your quarter call to the north.

- When you have finished your quarter call, if you have decided to use corresponding quarter candles, you may light the green quarter candle now.

- Continue in a clockwise direction to the Eastern Quarter. Raise your arms in a salute to the east, and then return to your altar.

- **Consecration:** You may use the example provided or write your own.

> We yearn for light and warmth on Winter Solstice, the longest night of the year. The word solstice means, "sun stop." The ancients realized that at Winter Solstice the sun reaches its lowest point in the sky. For three days after the solstice, the sun appears not to move from its recognized point on the horizon. On the 25th, it rises yet again, promising longer days as we move into the light. This is our history as mirrored in the Wheel of Life. It is the cycle of the Sun. For Wiccans, the cycle symbolizes the Child of Promise and Light.
>
> Promise means to pledge, to provide, or to do something. As the Wheel turns, the earth keeps her pledge to us with the promise of Spring, light, and life. These are her blessings and her gifts. What of us? What is our promise? What is our pledge? It is upon this that we should reflect, for we owe it to the life we are given to give something back.

Use the space provided to write your consecration.

- **Bringing power to the circle**

   Stand before your altar. Envision silver-white rays of moonlight
   entering your Crown Chakra as you chant:

   "Lady Light, Lady Night, fill me with power and energy this rite.

   Lord of Sacrifice, Lord of the Land, let my work be by your hand."

Circle the altar and repeat the chant several times until you feel the energy in the circle increase.

- **Invitation to The God and Goddess**

  "Holly King, Oak King, Lord of Light join us in this sacred rite.

  Maiden, Mother, Goddess Crone be with us on this sacred night."

- Light the gold candle (god), followed by the silver candle (goddess).

- **The Message**

  Consider this *The Gathering*, for you find me in all of my aspects. I am Maiden, witness to life. I am Mother, the giver of life, and I am Crone, the redeemer of life. As The Lord, I am the dying Holly King. I am the vital Oak King, and I am the Light of the Ways, The Child of Promise. We are gathered to witness the cycle and miracle of life. Consider your life a chalice to be filled once more. What will renew and restore you? With what will you toast? What will soothe your soul after long and weary days? I give you a recipe; use it and take what you need.

- **The Lesson:**

  Light the green candle in honor of The Child of Promise. Light the white candle for the Maiden. Light the red candle for the Mother, and the black candle for the Crone. Follow this recipe. Fill your life with these magickal ingredients.

1 part promise: write what you pledge to accomplish or become over the course of the year.

1 part hope: write what you hope to bring into the light for yourself and others.

1 part comfort: write where you will find your comfort and solace during times of trial.

1 part release: write what you surrender to the fires and forces of change.

Now, to each of the four quarters I send you. Journey at your pace, but make haste, for you must traverse the wheel. Heed my words.

To the East take your promise. Commune with the sylphs and ask their assistance to aid you in keeping your pledge. You will need the powers of intellect and communication.

Take your hope to the South. Commune with the power elementals, the mighty salamanders; masters of transformation. Ask for the passion, power, and will to fuel your hopes and dreams.

To the West you shall find consciousness. Take comfort with the undines. Ask that intuition guide you and that your conscience be your comfort and your counsel.

To The North, return to the home of the Mother. Release to her that which would cloud your cup. Give over any burden, so that it may be transformed in the cleansing nature of the Earth. Walk the circle now. When you have traversed the wheel, cast your recipes to the Cauldron. Use the black candle of the crone to light them. You may snuff the candles when you are ready.

- **Sharing**

Take time to feast and enjoy the circle you have cast. Ensure that you leave a sampling of the cakes and a taste of the beverage as an offering.

Closing the Circle

- Give thanks to The Lady and The Lord for their attendance. After thanking each, first snuff The Lord's candle, and then snuff The Lady's candle.

- Stand and move clockwise to the Eastern Quarter. Call to the guardians of the east and recite your quarter closing, offering thanks.

- Upon completion of your quarter closing, snuff the yellow candle and move clockwise (deosil) to the south.

- Standing in the Southern Quarter, call to the guardians of the south and offer your closing and thanks.

| |
| |
| |
| |
| |
| |
| |

- Upon completion of your quarter closing, snuff the red candle and

  move deosil to the west.

- Standing in the Western Quarter, call to the guardians of the west
  and thank them.

- Upon completion of your quarter closing, snuff the blue candle

  and move deosil to the north.

- Standing in the Northern Quarter, call to the guardians of the

  north and offer your closing and thanks.

Use the space provided.

| |
| |
| |
| |
| |
| |
| |

- Upon completion of your quarter closing, snuff the green candle and continue moving deosil to your altar.

- **Grounding**

  Take a moment to ground and close your chakras. Working from the Crown Chakra down to the root, envision the balls of light protected and covered.

- **Closing Chant**

  All energies attracted to this rite,

  depart now from this sacred site.

  Upon my will, and the words I have spoken, the circle is open, yet remains unbroken.

  Merry Meet, Merry Part, and Merry Meet again.

- **The Offering**

  Conclude your ritual by setting out the offering and returning your tools to the appropriate place.

Every act of ritual is an integration of the spirit with the Self.

Notes of a Priestess

Chapter 9

The Silver Path

Dedication and Initiation Ceremonies

Our path is a life-long journey. It is filled with twists and surprises. Our traveling companions are joy, blessings, and sorrow. The wonder of the Wiccan Way is that as we take this beautiful journey, we are never alone. The Lady and The Lord, in all of their aspects, are our guides and protectors. The elements and elementals are fierce guardians and friends. At this point in our studies, we arrive at a crossroads. Dedicate or initiate? Which one, and why?

Let's first address dedication. Dedicating allows one-year-and-one day to consider whether or not the path is right for you. Although you can always push yourself away from the table, so to speak, allowing yourself the time to experience how solitary or coven work suits is often

preferable to plunging into the work of a priest or priestess straight off.

In my tradition, all prospective coven members must dedicate. This

works well, because as dedicants they are allowed to attend circles and

participate in the energy of the coven. They learn the initial workings

and structure of craft and coven work. Additionally, they have an

opportunity to see if they are right for the coven and if the coven is right

for them. Dedicants learn the foundation and fundamental lessons that

are crucial to successful initiation as a priestess or priest of The Craft.

Each one of their elders followed the same path and is there to guide,

teach, and encourage them along the way. Initiation performed by

oneself or through the coven is a privilege and it must be earned.

Consider the fact that if you were to self-initiate, you would still need to

learn what to do and how to do it.

I caution everyone to be wary of a cooperative group or

organizational structure that allows you to begin at the top. If you are

anxious to start your own coven, you must establish workable

guidelines and an organizational flow that is in line with the tenets of

The Craft. How will you do this? How will you teach? What will you

require of your students and members of the coven? If you have come

this far in your reading, you are already ahead where your studies are
concerned. However, reading is not application. With all of the lessons,
rituals, and magickal applications contained within this book, it would
easily take you over one-year-and-one-day to effectively apply them all.
It really becomes a matter of allowing the knowledge to penetrate. As
you integrate the information, adapting your lifestyle and way of
thinking to the practice of Wicca becomes second nature. The
information that follows outlines the path of study for the dedicant.

- **Divination**. It is important that witches hone at least one means
  of divination. This requires research as well as trial and error.
  Begin with what interests you and see if you have an aptitude for
  it. There are various means of divination from cultures around the
  world. Your investment should be one of time and research as
  you tailor your means of divination to suit your innate talents.

- **Skill or craft**. Honing a craft or familiarization with fashioning
  tools is a definite requirement. Some covens require that their
  members make *some or all* of their magickal tools. Skills can range
  from sewing to welding or blacksmithing, depending upon your
  interest. Cooking and craftwork are also integral to the studies of
  a witch. To become skilled in any of these arenas requires an

investment of time. If you are already proficient at divination, or any of the aforementioned skills, then your next step is to apply them to your daily life and in service to The Craft.

♦ **History of The Old Religion**. Know your history, the origins of not only your practice, but that of shamanism and witchcraft in general. The study of anthropology, mythology, world cultures, and religions enriches your understanding of the Old Religion's place in a New Age. Modern Wicca is a melding of disciplines, peoples, and cultures.

♦ **World Myth**. Mythology is an essential aspect of study. As you integrate the practice of Wicca into your life, you will come across various pantheons. Understanding the creation myths, as well as the myths concerning the world's religions, deepens your understanding of your practice and of all practices. Libraries and local colleges can provide invaluable resources, as can DVDs such as the Joseph Campbell series on myths.

♦ **Herbalism and wort cunning**. Whether you take university courses, continuing education, or public classes it is important to not only read about the different uses and applications of herbs, but also to receive hands-on instruction in identification and application of herbs for medicinal and magickal use.

♦ **Aromatherapy application and Incense**. Courses in aromatherapy, use and application of essential oils, and the making and blending of incense are also crucial. Much can be gained from reading competent instructional manuals, but again, nothing will replace hands-on instruction with a qualified instructor or mentor.

♦ **Craft specific studies**. Along with a strong base of knowledge, today's witch must also possess a solid background in craft specific studies. Issues such as magick and the application and ethics of spell-work, the tables of correspondence, circle casting, and many of the subjects touched upon in this primer are considered craft specific studies, but the list doesn't end here. An understanding of astrology, numerology, tarot, and mysticism can prove invaluable.

♦ **Familiarization with the Wiccan community and Pagan culture**. Many witches begin their studies alone with little, if any, sense of community. Dedicants should use their time of study to research Wiccan churches, covens, and pagan communities. If you are interested in working with a group, or forming one of your own, it is essential that you use your time of study to find others of like mind. You want to ensure that the people you work with provide not only a sense of community, but are also a strong moral, ethical, and energetic match. Never join groups that ask you to participate in activities or ventures that are against your personal code. Finding the right fit may take time, but the benefits are more than worth the investment.

A Word about Magickal Names

Because many who elect to dedicate and/or initiate choose to do so under a magickal name, the researching of magickal names should be included in the seeker's studies. Once, a magickal name was essential to protect the identity of the witch from persecutors. A great many witches today practice The Craft under their magickal names for just that reason. There are many other reasons why one might select a magickal name. Some feel that using their magickal name in the practice of The Craft helps separate the mundane aspects of their lives from the magickal. Others like the idea of mystery, and still others believe that use of their magickal name during ritual or spell-work places them in the proper frame of mind to create magick. I am of the belief that your magickal name is sacred and should not be used with the same freedom as your given name. Your name holds power and meaning. The name that you choose, whether your given name, or magickal, is the name by which The Lady, The Lord, and all elements and elementals will know you. It is your bond, and a part of the seal of your magickal works. Perhaps it is not something that everyone is privy to. Should you choose to use a magickal name to identify yourself with The Craft, select a name that resonates with you. Its energy and meaning should complement you and your spiritual goals. The name may change and evolve as you do. It is better that the name grows with you, as opposed to something that you grow into. Every witch should know the history of her/his name, whether it is a birth name or a chosen name. It should be a source of pride and something that is a clear reflection of you.

Initiation

When you initiate into the practice of Wicca you are letting the Goddess, God, and the elements and elementals know that you are now working in service of The Craft. As a dedicant you have pledged to study the path and abide by the Rede. However, you have not undertaken the specific work necessary to initiate as a first-degree priest/ess and be noted as such. Initiation into The Craft means that you are in training to become a member of the Wiccan clergy. You are committing to learning and protecting the deeper mysteries. You are not obligated to complete all degrees, but you are making a conscious choice to follow the Wiccan path and work as a first-degree Initiate. That means taking on all the responsibilities and privileges of the position. There are those who are drawn to the cachet of the title *Priestess* or *Priest*. They view High Priestess or High Priest as the finishing point. Be very careful here. If your goal is status, recognition, or title hunting you are on the wrong path. Each role you play as you walk the Wiccan path is equally important. You will find that the farther along the path you walk, the more you serve. Recognition is not needed, nor desired as much, because you find fulfillment in service. Your deeds and your work, not your title, speak for you.

I cannot over-emphasize the responsibility aspect. Once you initiate, there's no room to claim ignorance of the novice. Whereas the path of the dedicant is one of study, the initiate both studies and serves. When you place yourself in service to The Lady and The Lord, your pledge is to them. You are expected to work in accordance with the Wiccan Rede: "An' it harm none, do what ye will." Moreover, your magick and general intent should be aligned with the greater good. And

of course, expect a big karmic whack if you knowingly act against the

Rede or interfere with the freewill of another.

Which choice is right for you? Take time to review the path of the

dedicant. Remember, you're looking at Wicca as a life path and practice.

Take the time you need. What's more, don't fool yourself into thinking

that you can skip over the studies and jump right into initiation and

service. Many people think that they have read and studied enough.

They don't have to pay their dues. What they don't realize is that the

practice and application of Wicca is a lifetime commitment to study. You

can't grow if you don't learn. The goal of Wiccan spirituality is continual

evolution for the self and soul, *and* for the world around you. I cannot

make the call for you as to where your starting point should be. I can

say that there are no shortcuts where your spirituality is concerned. If

you skip a step, I can guarantee that your lack of preparation will come

back to bite you. As for choices, I provide a Dedication/Path Blessing

ceremony. It is detailed in the same format as the sabbat rituals for

Chapter 8. This will ensure familiarity and also provide you with the

opportunity to write your own quarter calls as part of your dedication

ceremony. Take time to review the rite. After that, we can explore self-initiation and what to expect.

Path Blessing is a term used in my coven. For the purposes of this primer, you may use the terms dedication and path blessing interchangeably. Dedications/path blessings and initiations are best performed from February through May. This is because you are working in alignment with the correspondences. These rituals are symbolic of a fresh start. Spring through early summer (Beltane represents early summer on the Celtic calendar) is the traditional time frame for this type of work. If you discover The Craft and wish to dedicate outside of this time frame, don't worry! You can do one of two things.

- If you want to follow strict tradition, use the time in-between for study. Even once you dedicate, and perhaps more so, your path is one of study. Take the time to read, to compare, to reflect, and to learn.
- If you still feel you would be more comfortable dedicating, even if it is outside of the time frame, then adjust your intent to the season. If it occurs during the waning time of the year, ask The Lady, The Lord, and all good elements and elementals to aid in lessening the obstacles to your path. Ask them to grant you the

gifts of insight and introspection and for the ability to use this time of the waning year for such endeavors.

My mother coven did not allow dedications between August and November. However, my High Priestess did allow dedications to occur around the time of Yule, which is symbolic of new beginnings. I was lucky to be among those who dedicated at that time. It remains one of the most blessed days of my life.

Important Reminders

Before you begin the ceremony, *remember to prepare and take your ritual bath.* See Chapter 7 for a refresher ☺. Ensure that you have the required nine feet of white satin cord. This type of cord is also known as beading or rattail cord for necklaces. It can be found at most craft and sewing stores. The cord comprises the first cord of the **cingulum**, ritual cords worn in the manner of a belt around the waist. The cingulum is symbolic of our ties to God, Goddess, and The Craft. In my tradition the dedication, as well as each degree initiation, calls for a specific cord to be added and ultimately braided into the cingulum. Your first cord is white. It symbolizes your dedication, purity of intent, and the bones of our ancestors—our history. After you perform the ceremony, the cord should be worn each time you perform ritual. It is worn over your ritual robe or garment and is tied around the waist.

If you like, you can choose a gift to give yourself to commemorate your special day. Place your gift on the altar, unless you have gifted yourself with a robe or garment to wear for the occasion. This is your special ceremony. Treat it with care and consideration. Enjoy!

Dedication/Path Blessing

You will need:

♦ A work space or altar ideally facing the east or northeast

♦ (1) White sage bundle

♦ Frankincense and Myrrh resin with charcoal, or incense sticks

♦ An abalone shell or ash catcher

♦ Matches and/or a lighter

♦ (1) Small, white working candle

♦ (1) White feather (optional)

♦ (1) Silver candle for Goddess energy

♦ (1) Gold candle for God energy

♦ A dish of sea salt

- A dish of spring water

- Representation for the element of air

- Representation for the element of fire

- A drinking chalice or goblet

- (1) White candle for your dedication. A chime candle is fine

- (1) White satin cord, nine feet in length

- A beverage: Select a seasonally appropriate beverage. Wine or juice is fine. For spring and summer, consider white wine or a fruit juice like white grape or apple. For fall and winter, a red wine or grape juice will work nicely.

- Altar cakes. You may bake or purchase your altar cakes. Make your choice something you feel is appropriate for sharing with and offering to deity. I recommend light cakes like angel food.

Optional items:

- Corresponding colored candles and representations for each of the Four Quarters. 7-day devotional candles are recommended.

- Personal tools such as a wand or athame.

- God and goddess figures and/or altar representations

- Altar cloth

The Ceremony

Ensure that you have placed all of your Quarter representations in the appropriate quarter, and that all tools are readily available. Have the cakes ready on an altar plate and the beverage poured into the chalice. Take a seat before your altar. Begin by grounding and centering with the chakra visualization. Once you have accomplished this, you are ready to cast circle. Within the ritual, instructions and directions are noted in ( ) parentheses. All else should be spoken as directed.

Creating the circle:

- Using the sage, frankincense, and myrrh cast a Pagan Circle as you learned at the conclusion of Chapter 4.
- Once you have cast circle, return to the east. Pick up your representation of air, and hold it above your head. Invite the element and elementals of air to attend.

Use the worksheet provided for your quarter call to the east.

- When you have finished your quarter call, if you have decided to use corresponding quarter candles, you may light the yellow quarter candle now.

- Continue in a clockwise (deosil) direction to the Southern Quarter. Pick up your representation of fire, and hold it aloft.

Use the space provided for your quarter call to the south.

- When you have finished your quarter call, if you have decided to use corresponding quarter candles, you may light the red quarter candle now.

- Continue in a clockwise direction to the Western Quarter. Pick up your representation of water, and hold it aloft.

Use the space provided for your quarter call to the west.

| |
| |
| |
| |
| |
| |
| |
| |

- When you have finished your quarter call, if you have decided to use corresponding quarter candles, you may light the blue quarter candle now.

- Continue in a clockwise direction to the Northern Quarter. Pick up your representation of earth, and hold it aloft.

Use the space provided for your quarter call to the north.

- When you have finished your quarter call, if you have decided to use corresponding quarter candles, you may light the green quarter candle now.

- Continue in a clockwise direction to the Eastern Quarter. Raise your arms in a salute to the east, and then return to your altar.

- **Consecration:** You may use the example provided or write your own.

On this day, with the love of The Lady and the light of The Lord, I dedicate myself to the Wiccan path.

- **Bringing power to the circle**

  Stand before your altar. Envision silver-white rays of moonlight entering your Crown Chakra as you chant:

  "Silver Lady, Lady Bright, fill me with power and energy this rite.

Lord of Light, Lord of the Land, let my work be by your hand."

Circle the altar and repeat the chant several times until you feel the energy in the circle increase.

- **Invitation to The God and Goddess**

  "Oak King, whose light is the Sun, I call upon your energy that we may be one. Lady of Fire, Lady of Light, rise, come and be one with, (your name), this rite."

- Light the gold candle (god), followed by the silver candle (goddess).

- **The Ritual**

  The Path Blessing

  I, (your name), have thought upon the path I wish to take and have chosen wisely and well. From this day forward, I choose to dedicate myself to walking the path of The Lady and The Lord. I choose to study and to honor the tenets, sabbats, and ways of the wise. I shall abide by the Wiccan Rede, "an' it harm none, do what ye will." I shall not abuse the knowledge I gain, nor use this knowledge to interfere with the freewill of another.

Never shall I reveal any personal information about others who may share my path without their express permission. Never shall I reveal the sacred mysteries of The Craft, except to those who have made these promises as I have. I promise to be a guardian of the ways of the wise.

(Light the white candle upon your altar)

Before The Lady, The Lord, and all good elements and elementals, I do state my intent. I, *(your name),* do wish to be dedicated to the Mighty Ones and to The Craft, that I may learn of them, and that when I am ready, initiate to work in the ways of The Lady and The Lord. My path is one of study and devotion. May I walk in these ways, know myself, and bask in the light and blessings of the Mighty Ones.

Gracious Goddess, Gracious God, I ask this of you. May I find your love within and without. May I walk in perfect love and perfect trust. May I work to be true to The Rede and honor you, The Craft, and myself. Bless me, Mother. For, I am thy child. So Mote it be.

(Begin in the east. Walk to each of the Quarters, so that the Guardians shall know thee by name.)

East:

> Guardians of the Watchtowers of the east, mighty Paralda and elementals of air, (your name), stands before you now. I ask that as long as I honor and work within the ways of The Craft, that you grant me your presence and magickal gifts when I call upon you.

South:

> Guardians of the Watchtowers of the south, mighty Djinn and elementals of fire, (your name), stands before you now. I ask that as long as I honor and work within the ways of The Craft, that you grant me your presence and magickal gifts when I call upon you.

West:

> Guardians of the Watchtowers of the west, mighty Niksa and elementals of water, (your name), stands before you now. I ask that as long as I honor and work within the ways of

The Craft, that you grant me your presence and magickal gifts when I call upon you.

North:

Guardians of the Watchtowers of the north, mighty Gob and elementals of earth, (your name), stands before you now. I ask that as long as I honor and work within the ways of The Craft, that you grant me your presence and magickal gifts when I call upon you.

(Return to the east, facing your altar. Stand with your arms outstretched toward the heavens, feet slightly apart.) This is the position of Drawing Down the Moon.

I align my spirit with the energies of the heavens. I am a child of the goddess and I am loved. All good spirits take note that, (your name), stands before you this day.

(Return to your altar and take up your cingulum. Tie it around your waist.)

This cord represents the purity of my intent and lovingly binds me to The Lady and The Lord. May I ever walk in the light of their blessings.

(Sit before your altar. Snuff your white candle. You may light it and use it whenever you perform ritual or meditation.)

- **Sharing**

  Take time to feast and enjoy the circle you have cast. Ensure that you leave a sampling of the cakes and a taste of the beverage as an offering.

Closing the Circle

- Give thanks to The Lady and The Lord for their attendance. After thanking each, first snuff The Lord's candle, and then snuff The Lady's candle.
- Stand and move clockwise to the Eastern Quarter. Call to the guardians of the east and recite your quarter closing, offering thanks.

Use the space provided

- Upon completion of your quarter closing, snuff the yellow candle and move clockwise (deosil) to the south.

- Standing in the Southern Quarter, call to the guardians of the south and offer your closing and thanks.

Use the space provided

| |
| |
| |
| |
| |
| |
| |

- Upon completion of your quarter closing, snuff the red candle and move deosil to the west.

- Standing in the Western Quarter, call to the guardians of the west and thank them.

Use the space provided.

- Upon completion of your quarter closing, snuff the blue candle and move deosil to the north.

- Standing in the Northern Quarter, call to the guardians of the north and offer your closing and thanks.

Use the space provided.

- Upon completion of your quarter closing, snuff the green candle and continue moving deosil to your altar.

- **Grounding**

  Take a moment to ground and close your chakras. Working from the Crown Chakra down to the root, envision the balls of light protected and covered.

- **Closing Chant**

  All energies attracted to this rite,

  depart now from this sacred site.

Upon my will, and words I have spoken, the circle is open, yet remains unbroken.

Merry Meet, Merry Part, and Merry Meet again.

- **The Offering**

Conclude your ritual by setting out the offering and returning your tools to the appropriate place.

Congratulations! You have dedicated to The Craft.

***

A word about self-Initiation

If you have come this far in your studies, you are well on your way. Initiation and candidacy for degrees do not encompass the scope of this primer. I strongly urge you to continue your studies. If you would like to advance along the path of Wiccan study and coven membership, I invite you to contact me. As previously mentioned, the mysteries of Wiccan tradition are not revealed to the uninitiated. However, I do offer classes through my coven, The Circle of The Silver Path. Approved students are eligible for initiation and coven membership upon the successful conclusion of their coursework.

Training under my tutelage is rigorous. There are no shortcuts.

The curriculum includes research, writing, and online skype and class

sessions. You will be held accountable for all assignments. If you are

interested, contact me at: LadyKaliTara@gmail.com

Supplemental CD and Spirit Stones can be ordered from the e-mail

address listed above.

The supplemental CD includes audio guided visualizations with prompts

and is available for $ 5.95 + shipping and handling.

Spirit Stones include (10) hand selected semi-precious tumbled stones

with pouch and reference chart for $12.00 + cost of shipping and

handling.

Prices are subject to change with availability and market fluctuations.

Merry meet, Merry part, and Merry meet again!

Lady Kali Tara

Appendix

Yule Tree Blessing

You will need:

- Salt

- Benzoin

- Distilled water

- A small, glass bowl

- Frankincense resin

- Myrrh resin

- (1) Censer

- (1) White chime candle

- (1) Charcoal tablet for burning incense

- (1) Mortar and pestle for grinding the resin

Directions:

Add (3) pinches of sea salt and (1) pinch of Benzoin to the small bowl. Pour a moderate amount of distilled or spring water into the bowl. Stir the mixture lightly with your index finger. This is the purification water. Put the mixture aside. Next, grind one scoop each of frankincense and myrrh in the mortar and pestle. Ensure that you grind it fine enough so that it can be sprinkled onto the charcoal. Once ground, put the mixture aside. When all ingredients are prepared, place the charcoal on the censer. You will light the charcoal only when you are ready to perform the ceremony.

The Ceremony

Circling the tree in a clockwise direction. Lightly sprinkle the purification water on the tree's branches. As you do so, state:

With earth and water, I bless this tree.

Put away the purification water. Sprinkle the blended resin on the lit incense charcoal. Moving clockwise once more, circle the tree. As you wave the smoke toward the tree state:

With fire and air, I bless this tree.

Light the white candle. Stand before the tree and state:

By this light, and in friendship, I welcome this noble tree into my home. May it symbolize prosperity and hope in the coming year. May my endeavors be fertile. Noble tree, symbol of life and promise, I welcome thee in love. Blessed be.

SELECTED BIBLIOGRAPHY

Conway, D.J. *Celtic Magic*. St. Paul: Llewellyn, 1990.

Cunningham, Scott. *Cunningham's Encyclopedia of Magical Herbs*.

St. Paul: Llewellyn 2008.

Eason, Cassandra. *The Illustrated Directory of Healing Crystals*. London:

Collins and Brown 2004.

Farrar, Janet and Stewart. *A Witches Bible Compleat*. New York:

Magickal Childe Publishing 1995.

Federation of American Societies for Experimental Biology. "Burning

Incense Is Psychoactive: New Class Of Antidepressants Might Be

Right Under Our Noses." *Science Daily*, 20 May 2008. Web.13

November 2008.

Filan, Kenaz. *The Haitian Vodou Handbook: Protocols for Riding with the

Lwa*. Rochester: Destiny Books 2007.

Guiley, Rosemary Ellen. *The Encyclopedia of Witches and Witchcraft*.

New York: Facts on File 1989.

Heaven, Ross. *Vodou Shaman: The Haitian Way of Healing and Power.*
Rochester: Destiny Books 2003.

Irvin, Jan and Andrew Rutajit. *Astrotheology & Shamanism: Christianity's Pagan Roots.* Gnostic Media Research and Publishing 2009.

Judith, Anodea. *Wheels of Life.* St. Paul: Llewellyn 1995.

Mégemont, Florence. *The Metaphysical Book of Gems and Crystals.*
Rochester: Healing Arts Press 2003.

Müller-Ebeling, Claudia, Christian Rätsch, and Wolf-Dieter Storl.
Witchcraft Medicine. Rochester: Inner Traditions 1998.

Solomon, Maria. *Helping Yourself with Magickal Oils A-Z.* New York:
Original Publications 1997.

Starhawk. *The Spiral Dance: A Rebirth of the Ancient Religion of The Great Goddess.* San Francisco: Harper Collins 1989.

Sullivan, Tammy. *Elemental Witch.* St. Paul: Llewellyn 2006.

ABOUT THE AUTHOR

Lady Kali Tara is a Haitian-American High Priestess of two covens, each with its own recognized tradition. She holds a Masters in Education and has worked as a spiritual counselor and reader for over 20 years. *Teachings of an Outlaw Witch* is the natural extension of an exciting spiritual journey that has led her to travel and study with shamans throughout the world. Whether lecturing in college classrooms or leading workshops at spiritual centers, Lady Kali Tara shares a tradition of Wicca that can become a lifelong practice of spirituality to nurture the mind, nourish the body, and feed the soul. She lives and practices with her husband in Ashland, Oregon.

www.ingramcontent.com/pod-product-compliance
Lightning Source LLC
Chambersburg PA
CBHW021044090426
42738CB00006B/178

9 780615 745404